JUICING FOR BEGINNERS

How to Make Natural and Effective Drinks to Slim your Waistline and Improve Your Body Health | A Simple and Tasty Method for your Wellness

NATHALIE OLSON

TABLE OF CONTENTS

Introduction

Juicing has been proven to be an effective method for weight loss and body detoxification. However, some individuals are hesitant to try it due to concerns about the cost and time commitment. This informative book not only highlights the numerous benefits of juicing but also offers a variety of delicious recipes to try. Whether you're a seasoned juicer or a beginner, this book is an excellent resource for anyone looking to improve their health and well-being.

Juicing is considered a good way to lose weight, but it can also be expensive because of the equipment and time it takes. This book will discuss how juicing can be beneficial, but there are many other ways to achieve the same benefits without spending so much money.

The key advantage of juicing is that you get more out of what you put in compared to other methods. By using a juicer and eating the juices instead of replacing the fiber in your diet with packaged foods, you will lose weight and feel better overall. The juice provides better nutrition than if you just replaced your meals with juice, plus they are packed with vitamins, minerals, and antioxidants which make them highly nutritious. Juicing is also supposed to be an optimal way to cleanse your body and increase energy, but this method is only recommended for ten days. You should also be cautious of juice cleanses because many of them are just fruit and vegetable juice mixes and not cleansers. Juices might help you lose weight, but if they aren't done properly, they can cause more harm than good.

Thanks to juices, you will get the nutrients in vegetables and fruits without having to eat them, which makes them easy to digest. The process extracts all the necessary vitamins and minerals from vegetables along with antioxidants and enzymes that you wouldn't be able to get by eating them. Juicing can also help you lose weight because fruits & vegetables are high in fiber which helps your body digest slowly, allowing you to eat less while still feeling full.

Basics of Juicing

WHAT IS JUICING?

To extract their juice, fresh fruit and or vegetables are often ground, squeezed, or pressed during the juicing process. The method of pressing newly picked fruits to get immediate access to the nutrients in such fruits is known by its more contemporary name, cold pressing.

The practice of juicing had its origins in the 1920s and 1930s, but the 1970s were the decade in which it took off as a craze. By the 1990s, healthy eating and juice bars were becoming more commonplace among the general population.

Fresh juice is a simple method to get various nutrients, including vitamins and minerals. However, despite the fact that even though evidence supports juicing, the possible health benefits might vary greatly depending on the specific ingredients that are used to make the juice. If you aren't cautious, you could consume an unhealthy number of calories and sugar via the beverages you drink.

BENEFITS OF JUICING

It can be fun, safe, and easy to live a happier and healthier life when juicing is done the right way. There are a lot of possible health benefits to juice, and you might enjoy them if you make this process a regular part of your life.

WEIGHT LOSS

Juicing has long been touted as a natural and effective way to aid in weight loss. Freshly squeezed juices contain high levels of vitamins, minerals and antioxidants that are essential for health and also work to detoxify the body. Vegetable-based juices are especially beneficial as they provide vital nutrients while being low in calories. When consumed instead of processed or high-calorie drinks, juicing can help reduce overall calorie intake which ultimately leads to weight loss. Additionally, freshly prepared juice contains dietary fiber which helps keep you feeling full for extended periods of time, reducing the likelihood of overeating. Incorporating regular juicing into a balanced diet is a highly effective means to help support overall wellbeing and achieve sustainable weight loss goals. However, it should be noted that juicing alone should not be considered a complete solution and must be combined with other healthy lifestyle choices such as physical activity and adequate sleep for maximum benefits.

ANTI-AGING

Juicing is an incredibly easy and effective way to incorporate anti-aging benefits into a healthy lifestyle. These benefits include increased energy, improved digestion, clearer skin, and better cognitive function. By juicing fruits and vegetables, you are able to consume a higher amount of essential vitamins, minerals and antioxidants to support your body's natural processes that fight the signs of aging. Vegetables like spinach or kale are great sources of vitamin C which helps collagen production - this keeps skin looking youthful and firm. Pomegranate juice contains polyphenols which help prevent cell damage caused by sun exposure. Other examples are beets which contain betalain pigments that can reduce inflammation throughout the body – inflammation is linked with aging skin such as fine lines and wrinkles. With regular juicing habits, these beneficial compounds may slow down the aging process in various ways for an overall healthier appearance!

DETOX AND CLEANSING

Juicing is an excellent method to detox and cleanse your body. When you juice, you're removing the pulp and fiber from fruits and vegetables, which allows your digestive system to break down the nutrients more easily. This means that your body can absorb all of the vitamins, minerals, and antioxidants in one quick shot. Juicing also gives your body a rest from having to work hard to break down solid food, allowing it to focus on flushing out toxins instead. Additionally, certain juices like lemon or ginger can help stimulate digestion and reduce inflammation in the body. Overall, adding fresh juices to your diet can bring numerous health benefits including clearer skin, better digestion, increased energy levels and an overall improved sense of well-being.

ENERGIZING

Juicing has been touted as an effective way to boost energy levels due to the high concentration of nutrients and vitamins found in fresh fruits and vegetables. When producing juice, the fibrous pulp is removed, making it easier for the body to absorb the nutrients and quickly provide a burst

of energy. Juicing also keeps blood sugar level steady by avoiding sudden spikes commonly associated with processed foods or sugary drinks that can lead to crashes later on. Moreover, juicing provides hydration which is another vital factor behind feeling alert and energized.

ANTI-INFLAMMATORY

The popularity of juicing has increase as a means of enhancing health and addressing inflammation in the body. The benefits of juicing for reducing inflammation are significant, as fresh fruits and vegetables contain high levels of antioxidants which help to counterbalance free radicals in the body. These free radicals can impact inflammation, leading to a range of chronic conditions like arthritis, heart disease, and some kinds of cancer. Juicing also provides a powerful dose of nutrients that are quickly absorbed into the bloodstream, helping the body to repair damaged tissues and boost immune function. By incorporating juicing into a daily routine, individuals can significantly reduce inflammation levels in their bodies by flooding their system with anti-inflammatory compounds found in fresh produce.

IMMUNE BOOSTER

Immune boosters such as ginger, turmeric, and citrus fruits are packed with vitamins, antioxidants and anti-inflammatory compounds that help care the body's natural defense system. Juicing these ingredients can increase absorption of these nutrients and provide a quick and easy way to eat multiple servings of fruits & vegetables in one serving.

DIGESTION

Juicing has increasingly gained popularity as a solution to improve digestion. As opposed to solid food, juicing allows the body to rapidly absorb essential vitamins, minerals, and enzymes reducing digestion time. Moreover, with regular intake of fresh fruits and vegetables in the form of juices, one is more likely to consume an adequate amount of fiber which effectively keeps bowel movements regular, significantly improving constipation. The digestion process becomes easier and efficient leading to quick absorption of essential nutrients into the bloodstream. Additionally, juicing promotes healthy gut bacteria by providing prebiotic fiber that builds a supportive environment for beneficial digestive flora ultimately strengthening the immune system.

JUICING VS EATING RAW FRUITS AND VEGETABLES

Registered dieticians and other health-care professionals are divided on the issue of whether or not juicing is more beneficial than eating raw fruits and vegetables. While juicing certainly isn't unhealthy, there is some debate as to whether it is healthier than just eating the fruits and vegetables themselves. As many detractors of the juicing trend are keen to point out, however, a significant portion of the fiber content of fruits and vegetables is lost during the juicing process.

In order to understand the differences between juicing and eating raw fruits and vegetables, you need to know the basics about how a juicer works. A juicer is a kitchen appliance that takes the work out of extracting the juice from fresh fruits and vegetables. These devices are motor-operated, and they come in a variety of sizes. Though the mechanics of different models may vary, most juicers require you to push the raw fruits and vegetables through a feed tube. Inside, the appliance extracts the juice from the plant fibers, separating out the seeds, skin, and pulp. The fresh juice then exits the machine through a spout and into the desired glass or container.

For many people, making use of a juicer is a quick & easy way to boost the daily intake of fruits and vegetables. While it is true that some of the fiber content of the raw fruits and vegetables is lost during juicing, there are many unique benefits that juicing provides over eating raw fruits and vegetables. These include:

- Juicing is an excellent alternative if you do not normally like eating raw fruits and vegetables.
- The results are delicious - you can even disguise the flavor of vegetables by combining them with your favorite fruits.
- Juicing is a quick and easy process; the resulting juice can be taken with you for an on-the-go meal.
- Adding some of the pulp to your pressed juice will help restore some of its fiber content.
- Juicing does not require you to peel or chop the produce before using it (depending on the type of juicer you buy).
- Homemade juices have a fresh-squeezed taste; store-bought juices simply can't compare.
- Juicing is a great way to help your kids get the vitamins and minerals they need from fruits and vegetables.
- Leftover pulp from juicing can be used in baked goods, such as muffins, or as a base for homemade stocks and broths.

- Juicing is an economical way to make use of fruits and vegetables that are about to spoil.

JUICING VS BLENDING

If you have never juiced before you may be wondering how it works, or how it compares to blending.

Juicing uses a machine called a JUICER, while blending, as in making smoothies, uses a BLENDER. They are not the same.

Blending foods in a blender to make smoothies is also very healthy, because blending foods breaks down the cell walls of the food, which releases enzymes, and allows your body to absorb the nutrients much easier. This skips the first step in digestion and saves a big energy drain on the body. Digestion is a HUGE energy thief from the body!

Juicing, on the other hand, requires a juicing machine. As you put the fresh produce into a juicer, it turns fresh, raw food into a delicious liquid juice to give your body a boost of super-power health!

Juicing extracts the phytonutrients, minerals and vitamins from the food and gives you a pure refreshing juice! These nutrients are loaded in your liquid drink. You can almost FEEL the power the moment you drink it!

As the juicer extracts these micronutrients into a juice, it spits the 'pulp' out the other side into a container. This is one difference between juicing and blending. The pulp is the fiber in the food. By removing the pulp, you are able to immediately absorb these powerful nutrients into your body, without needing to digest the pulp.

Remember, digestion is a huge energy drain! Removing pulp allows instant absorption of a super condensed version of vitamins, minerals, enzymes and micronutrients. You could take a huge platter of food and juice it down into one tasty glass. Could you imagine EATING all of that food? Probably not! But you could drink it, in one glass.

Drinking a glass of juice is like eating a bushel of fresh raw food in one small glass!

These nutrient dense juices retain the majority of vitamins, minerals, and phytonutrients found in fresh food, but in a much smaller package. And with the right mix, even vegetables that you never liked before taste good. You can simply 'sneak' them in to your juice mix!

This is a great way to consume foods you may not normally eat. If you are like me, there are quite a few veggies I rarely eat, but I add them into my juice, and sneak them into my diet. And fruits are loaded with health benefits too.

You will need a juicer to get started. The prices range from low to high, and are similar to the prices of a blender (from cheap to super good!) But any juicer will do. Some juicers give more yield from leafy greens, but even the most inexpensive juicer will create a delicious juice from the recipes in this book.

Making Your Juice

CHOOSING A JUICER

Choosing a juicer can be a confusing process if you don't already understand the basics. Before you go shopping for your new juicer, take the time to learn about the three different types so you can decide which option is best for you. The three main types of juicers are: centrifugal juicers, masticating juicers, and triturating juicers. Each type has its own list of pros and cons, so in order to select the right one for your situation, you need to think about what features you want. You should also decide what price range you are willing to consider, because juicers can be quite expensive.

CENTRIFUGAL JUICERS

This type of juicer has tiny teeth and a basket that spins quickly. These juicers will grind up fresh fruits and vegetables to make new and pulpy juice. The juice will then go through a sieve with a fine mesh. People often end up with a lot of foam in their juice glasses when they use centrifugal juicers. If you don't like foamy drinks, a centrifugal juicer might not be the best choice. Besides that, you'd have to drink the juice right away to keep the air from getting in it.

They are sometimes called "extractors" because of how they work. Another thing to think about is that this type of juicer makes a lot of waste. You'll have to throw the pulp away, which means you could waste a lot of fresh produce if you just throw it away. If you want to go organic, you might not be able to use a centrifugal juicer.

You'd better not throw away the pulp in your juice or use it for something else.

People who use centrifugal juicers can make a lot of noise. They make a lot of juice quickly. As long as you live on your own, this might not be a big deal. You may not like this juicer's noise if you have kids at home and want to make juice in the morning. You can use this juicer to make fruit smoothies like apples and carrots, but it might not be as good at making smoothies with leafy greens like kale and spinach. Centrifugal juicers are easy to use, light, and clean. After using the juicer, you can take it apart and put the parts that can be removed in your dishwasher. It's also a good thing about centrifugal juicers that they're usually the cheapest.

MASTICATING JUICERS

Masticating juicers get their name because of how they work, and they are called that because of that. Because these juicers have augers with sharp teeth made of metal, they look like fruits and vegetables are being chewed. When you use a centrifugal juicer, there is a lot of foam. Masticating juicers make very little foam, and they allow you to get the most liquid out of fresh produce, even from the pulp. When you use this type of juicer, you don't have to make a lot of juice. You can then store the liquid in your refrigerator. Centrifugal juicers work faster than these, but they don't work as quickly as they should.

They are also called "cold-press juicers," You can use them to juice kale, spinach, and other leafy greens. Besides being quiet, these types of juicers are also thought to be better at preserving the nutrients in the juice they make. There are more expensive masticating juicers than the other types, and if you want one with a powerful motor, you'll have to pay for it. If you don't like citrus fruits, this juicer isn't the best choice. It's also not very good at juicing low-water vegetables or fruits either.

TRITURATING JUICERS

Triturating juicers have twin gears that rotate to crush fresh produce then grind it into fine particles. These powerful gears work efficiently to extract most of the juice from your ingredients until you are left with dry pulp and high-quality, nutrient-dense juice. Triturating juicers are especially effective at extracting juice from leafy greens, hearty veggies, and soft fruits. This type of juicer is relatively quiet but they are often bigger and bulkier than other types of juicers.

One huge benefit of these types of juicers is that you can use them for other tasks too, like chopping vegetables or grinding nuts and seeds. Since the juicer comes with added features, it also comes at a higher price. But if you plan to make different types of juices regularly and you want a piece of equipment that you can use for other purposes, this type of juicer may be the best option for you.

FRUITS AND VEGETABLES FOR JUICING

HEALTHY FRUIT

Apple: Apples contain an antioxidant called quercetin, which helps to reduce LDL (bad) cholesterol levels. These fruits are also rich in a soluble fiber called pectin, which may help flush toxic heavy metals from the body.

Avocado: Avocados are an excellent source of heart-healthy fats (monounsaturated fats). In addition, avocados provide potassium to regulate blood pressure, vitamin K to promote bone health, and plant-based protein.

Banana: Bananas are rich in B vitamins, which help promote healthy sleep patterns and reduce mood swings and irritability. This fruit also provides plenty of vitamin C in addition to potassium and magnesium, all of which help to replenish the body's store of electrolytes. Bananas are also naturally sweet—they can be pureed and blended into any of your favorite juices.

Blackberry: In addition to being an excellent source of vitamin C, blackberries contain high levels of calcium, potassium, iron, and fiber. Berries like blackberries contain the highest levels of antioxidants of any fruit.

Black Cherry: Cherries are an excellent source of iron, which helps the body produce healthy blood cells. These fruits also contain an anti-cancer compound called ellagic acid, and have high levels of vitamins A and C. In addition to these nutrients, cherries also possess antioxidant, anti-inflammatory, and antibacterial properties.

Blood Orange: Blood oranges are a variety of orange known for their crimson-colored flesh. This unique color is due to high levels of anthocyanins, a type of antioxidant pigment—their presence makes blood oranges richer in antioxidants than other oranges. Blood oranges are also a good source of dietary fiber, vitamin C, calcium, and folate.

Blueberry: Like apples, blueberries contain pectin as well as flavonoids, which may help reduce your risk for type 2 diabetes. Blueberries are also rich in vitamin C, potassium, and tannins, which have antiviral and antibacterial properties. Additionally, blueberries contain manganese, which contributes to healthy bone growth.

Cantaloupe: Cantaloupes are round melons with a bright orange flesh that is bursting with nutrients. Though full of juice and sweet flavor, cantaloupe is low in calories, and an excellent source of folic acid, beta-carotene, fiber, potassium, and vitamin C. Unlike many fruits and vegetables, cantaloupe also contains complex B vitamins.

Grape: Grapes are rich in a number of vitamins, including A, B, and C, in addition to minerals such as calcium, iron, phosphorus, magnesium, potassium, and selenium. Grapes also contain flavonoids, a powerful antioxidant that can help repair damage caused by free radicals—this property makes grapes an excellent anti-aging aid.

Grapefruit: Like all citrus fruits, grapefruit is an excellent source of vitamin C. Grapefruit also contains limonene, a compound that may help reduce the risk of breast cancer. Additionally, grapefruits are a great source of soluble fiber, which may help lower unhealthy blood cholesterol levels.

Kiwi: Kiwi is a brilliant source of vitamin C, that aids to heal wounds and keep your teeth and gums healthy. These fruits also contain vitamin K, vitamin E, folate, copper, and potassium. The enzymes found in kiwi have been shown to soothe digestive issues and may reduce the appearance of wrinkles.

Lemon: Lemon is often referred to as the most powerful fruit for detoxification. It has been linked to cancer prevention, relief from digestive issues, and reduced risk for heart disease and stroke. Lemons are rich in calcium, magnesium, potassium, and phosphorus.

Lime: Limes are very similar to lemons in their nutritional properties. These fruits are a good source of vitamin C, vitamin B6, folate, and potassium. Limes also contain flavonoids, a powerful antioxidant, and various other phytonutrients.

Mango: Mangoes contain both vitamin A and vitamin C, which make them very beneficial for strengthening the immune system. Mangoes are a good source of potassium, which has been shown to regulate heart rate and blood pressure. They have also been linked to reduced risk for certain types of cancer.

Melon: Melons, such as honeydew and watermelon, possess both antioxidant and anti-cancer properties. These fruits contain adenosine, a naturally occurring chemical that may reduce the risk for cancer and stroke.

Orange: Oranges are known for their vitamin C content, but they actually contain more than 170 different phytonutrients. These fruits have been shown to help shrink tumors, prevent blood clots, and reduce inflammation.

Papaya: Papayas are known for their antioxidant and anti-cancer properties. These fruits contain powerful enzymes that help to reduce constipation and promote healthy digestion. Additionally, papayas are a good source of potassium and vitamins A and C.

Passion Fruit: Passion fruit is a very aromatic fruit with a unique flavor. They are an excellent source of dietary fiber, vitamin A, vitamin C, and beta-carotene. Passion fruit is also rich in potassium, which may help regulate blood pressure and reduce the risk for cardiovascular disease.

Peach: In addition to their sweet flavor, peaches are also known for being an excellent source of both vitamin A and potassium. These fruits also contain boron and niacin, or vitamin B3, which has been shown to reduce the risk for cardiovascular disease.

Pear: Pears are an excellent source of dietary fiber, vitamin C, boron, and potassium. These fruits have been used for a variety of benefits, including as a diuretic, a cleanser, and a digestive aid.

Pineapple: Pineapples are a good source of iron, potassium, and vitamin C. These fruits also contain bromelain and other anti-inflammatory compounds, which help to promote joint health. Pineapple has also been used as a natural diuretic and a mild laxative.

Pomegranate: Pomegranates are an excellent fruit for cleansing and detoxing the body. These fruits contain vitamin C, magnesium, potassium, and beta-carotene—they have also been identified as the third-highest fruit source of antioxidants. Pomegranates contain lycopene and other phytonutrients that may help reduce the risk for prostate cancer.

Raspberry: In addition to being rich in vitamins C, K, and E, raspberries also contain folate, manganese, copper, and iron. Raspberries have been shown to help lower LDL (bad) cholesterol and to inhibit the growth of certain cancers.

Strawberry: Like most berries, strawberries are a good source of vitamin C, which helps to heal wounds and improve gum and teeth health. Strawberries are also known to have antiviral, antioxidant, and anti-cancer properties. These berries have also been linked to lowering LDL (bad) cholesterol, suppressing colon cancer, and protecting against Alzheimer's disease.

Tangerine: Tangerines are a good source of calcium, copper, magnesium, potassium, and beta-carotene. These fruits also contain sulfur, which helps promote detoxification of the liver. Additionally, tangerines have been shown to have antibacterial, anti-cancer, diuretic, and decongestant properties.

HEALTHY VEGETABLES

Arugula: Arugula is a leafy green and a cruciferous vegetable, which means that it is rich in antioxidants and flavonoids that may help reduce your risk for cancer. Arugula is also a good source for vitamins A, C, and K and a variety of essential minerals.

Asparagus: Asparagus is an excellent source of folate, which is vital for fetal development. This vegetable is also packed with antioxidants, which have been shown to reduce the appearance of aging and to slow cognitive decline. Asparagus also contains dietary fiber, chromium, and vitamins A, C, E, and K.

Beet: Beets and beet greens are an excellent source of iron, choline, iodine, manganese, potassium, and vitamins A and C. Additionally, research has demonstrated that beets aid us in oxygenating the blood, enhancing performance while exercising.

Bell Pepper: Red, green, and yellow bell peppers contain high levels of vitamin C, which is essential for healing wounds and for maintaining eye and gum health. They also contain vitamin A, which is a key contributor to skin and eye health.

Bok Choy: A type of leafy Chinese cabbage, bok choy is rich in a variety of phytonutrients, vitamins, and minerals. This vegetable is a good source of antioxidants, which combined with fiber and various vitamins, makes bok choy an anti-cancer and cholesterol-reducing food.

Broccoli: Like arugula, broccoli is a cruciferous vegetable and an excellent source of dietary fiber. It contains vitamin C, which helps promote healing, as well as vitamin E, which may help reduce your risk for certain cancers. Broccoli is also rich in iron, potassium, calcium, selenium, zinc, and sulfur.

Brussels Sprout: These vegetables are rich in dietary fiber, folate, potassium, and manganese. In addition, the vitamin C and vitamin K content of only one cup of Brussels sprouts is sufficient to cover over one hundred % of the average person's required daily consumption for both nutrients. Brussels sprouts have been linked to cancer prevention and have also been shown to support detoxification.

Cabbage: Cabbage is one of few vegetables that naturally contain vitamin E. This vegetable is also rich in sulfur, which has been shown to help purify the blood and detoxify the liver. Cabbage also contains antibacterial, antioxidant, and anti-inflammatory properties.

Carrot: Carrots are one of the most readily available vegetables, and they are also incredibly rich in vitamins and minerals. Carrots are a great source of vitamins A, B, and C as well as iron, calcium, potassium, and sodium. Carrots also contain beta-carotene and carotenoids, which help reduce the risk for cancer, cardiovascular disease, and macular degeneration.

Cauliflower: Cauliflower is an extremely versatile vegetable that is also rich in a number of nutrients. High in B vitamins, phosphorus, potassium, manganese, and vitamin K, this vegetable is very nutrient dense. Cauliflower is also a good source of antioxidants as well as glucosinolates, which help support the liver's detox abilities.

Celery: A very low-calorie food, celery is rich in a variety of vitamins and minerals. The silicon content of celery helps to strengthen joints and bones, while iron and magnesium help support blood health. Celery has also been shown to have diuretic and anti-cancer properties.

Cilantro: Cilantro is an herb that is incredibly rich in antioxidants that can help lower your LDL (bad) cholesterol and raise your good (HDL) cholesterol levels. This herb contains numerous vitamins, including folic acid, niacin, beta-carotene, and vitamins A, C, and K. There is also research to suggest that cilantro may be beneficial in managing Alzheimer's disease.

Collard Greens: Collard greens are an excellent source of vitamin C, manganese, chlorophyll, and beta-carotene. They have both antioxidant and anti-cancer properties. They may also be the strongest of all vegetables in lowering unhealthy cholesterol levels.

Cucumber: Cucumbers are an excellent source of potassium and phytosterols, both of which help to lower cholesterol. These vegetables have a high-water content, which makes them great for juicing. They are also a good source of B vitamins and may help control blood pressure.

Dandelion Greens: Though it may sound odd to eat them, dandelion greens are actually incredibly healthy. These greens are an outstanding source of vitamin K, that assists to support blood and bone health. Dandelion greens also contain nutrients that contribute to liver and gallbladder health.

Fennel: Fennel is particularly beneficial for the digestive system. This herb contains calcium, folate, potassium, magnesium, phosphorus, iron, and copper. It is also a good source of vitamins C and B5.

Garlic: Garlic is known for its antimicrobial, antibiotic, and anti-cancer properties. This allium aids in lowering blood cholesterol levels and to adjust blood sugar. Garlic also comprises a diversity of vitamins, minerals, and antioxidants, that make it valuable for boosting the immune system.

Ginger: Ginger is an excellent food for detoxing—it cleanses the body and helps to support healthy digestion. Ginger also has antinausea, anti-inflammatory, and antioxidant properties.

Green Onion: Green onions are also called scallions or spring onions, and they contain a variety of vitamins and minerals as well as other phytochemicals. These vegetables contain vitamins K and C, which help to support bone health, as well as vitamin A for eye health. Green onions are also a good source of various phytochemicals like quercetin and anthocyanins, which boost immune system health.

Kale: Kale is the highest vegetable source of vitamin K, which may help reduce the risk for certain cancers. This leafy vegetable is also a good source of calcium, iron, chlorophyll, and vitamins C and A. Kale is very nutrient dense, providing many healthy minerals, including iron, potassium, phosphorus, and manganese.

Mint: Mint is an herb that helps to soothe both indigestion and inflammation—its scent alone can stimulate the salivary glands, encouraging the production of enzymes that aid digestion. Mint is also a good source of plant-based omega-three fatty acids, which support healthy hair, skin, and nails.

Parsley: This herb is one of the highest natural sources for vitamin C. Parsley is rich in folate, which helps to prevent certain cancers and may also improve heart health. It also has diuretic properties, which means that it helps the body flush excess water.

Parsnip: Parsnips are known for their anti-cancer and anti-inflammatory properties. These vegetables contain high levels of vitamins C and E as well as protein, iron, and calcium. Parsnips have also been used as a natural diuretic and detoxifier.

Pumpkin: Pumpkin has been shown to reduce inflammation and may also reduce your risk for prostate cancer. This vegetable is high in vitamins C and E as well as copper, iron, and potassium. The phytochemicals present in pumpkin have also been shown to have a favorable effect on insulin and glucose levels in diabetes lab models.

Radish: Radishes are the roots of cruciferous vegetables, and they are an excellent source of vitamins and minerals. The leaves of the plant contain more protein, calcium, and vitamin C than the roots, and they have often been used to fight cancer, treat kidney problems, and soothe skin irritation. Radishes are also rich in vitamin C, folic acid, and anthocyanins, which make them effective as a cancer-fighting food.

Romaine Lettuce: While some lettuces (like iceberg) are fairly low in nutrients, that is not the case with romaine lettuce. This lettuce is incredibly rich in vitamins A, K, and C as well as potassium, iron, magnesium, and manganese.

Spinach: Spinach is a great source of vitamins A, C, and E, and it also contains high levels of calcium, iron, potassium, and protein. Additionally, spinach contains choline, a B-complex vitamin which supports healthy cognitive function. The iron content in spinach helps to build healthy blood cells.

Summer Squash: Summer squash is very low in calories but rich in vitamins. These vegetables contain vitamins C and A as well as magnesium, copper, riboflavin, and phosphorus. Summer squash is also a good source of antioxidants, which help to repair damage from free radicals.

Sweet Potato: Sweet potatoes have been identified as beneficial for eye health, detoxification, and digestive support. High in copper, iron, magnesium, manganese, and other nutrients, sweet potatoes also have anti-cancer properties.

Swiss Chard: A leafy green vegetable, Swiss chard (and other chards), is considered one of the healthiest vegetables available. Chards are rich in dietary fiber and protein in addition to containing high levels of vitamins A, K, and C.

Tomato: Tomatoes are an excellent source of vitamin C, potassium, copper, iron, and magnesium. They are recognized to contain over nine thousand phytonutrients, including the antioxidant lycopene, which has been linked to cancer prevention and improved mental and physical health.

Zucchini: Zucchini is a good source of copper, iron, magnesium, manganese, phosphorus, potassium, and vitamin C. This vegetable is also a good source of vitamin A and niacin (vitamin B3), which has been linked to reduced risk for cardiovascular disease.

PREPARATIONS AND PRECAUTIONS FOR JUICES

Though juicing provides many benefits, there are a few precautions you should be aware of before starting a juicing regimen:

- Clean your fruits & vegetables thoroughly before juicing. This is especially important if you are using produce that is not organic. You may want to use a vegetable wash to ensure it is free of dirt, pesticides, and other contaminants.
- Make sure to use only fresh produce for juicing. If you are using frozen fruits or vegetables, thaw them before you juice them.
- Cut the produce into small, uniform pieces before juicing. This will make it easier to juice and ensure you get the maximum amount of juice out of the produce.
- If you are using a juicer, read the instructions carefully before use.
- Make sure to keep the juicing machine clean and debris-free. After each use, clean the blades and other parts of the machine thoroughly.
- If you are using a manual juicer, use a cutting board and wear protective gloves to avoid any injuries.
- Use a filter to remove any pulp or chunks of produce from the juice.
- Make sure to drink the juice immediately after it is made. If you plan to store it, make sure to store it in a glass container and keep it refrigerated.

Juicing is an effective way to increase the nutrition in your diet and foster healthier choices. But it's not a magic bullet. Getting yourself some amazing collection of juicing recipes like the ones in this book will be your first step to an exciting way of providing yourself with a full-scale of vitamins, minerals, nutrients, and other microelements and shedding all your excess weight like you never had it. These recipes are tested, nutrient-rich combinations of fruits and vegetables that will help you reach your health goals, you do not have to speculate.

TIPS ON CLEANING AND STORING

JUICING EQUIPMENT

Cleaning and storing juicing equipment is an important part of maintaining the longevity and functionality of your equipment. B are some tips to help you clean and store your juicing equipment:

1. Unplug the juicer and disassemble all parts before cleaning.

2. Rinse the parts under hot water immediately after juicing to prevent pulp and other debris from drying on the surface of the parts.

3. When cleaning the parts, opt for a soft-bristled brush or sponge and refrain from using abrasive materials such as steel wool or harsh cleaning chemicals, as they can cause damage to the equipment.

4. When dealing with tough stains, you may opt to utilize a blend of water and baking soda or water and white vinegar to scrub the components.

5. Dry the parts thoroughly before storing them to prevent mold and bacteria growth. Use a clean towel or air dry the parts for a few hours.

6. Store the parts in a clean and dry location. Keep the juicer covered to prevent dust and debris from accumulating on the surface.

7. Regularly check the parts for signs of wear and tear. Replace any damaged or worn-out parts to ensure the equipment is functioning properly.

HOW TO KEEP JUICES FRESH

Juice made in a centrifugal juicer should be consumed immediately, or at least very soon after juicing. Centrifugal juicers whip air into the juice, speeding oxidation and the breakdown of beneficial phytonutrients.

Juice made in a masticating or a triturating juicer can generally be safely stored for 24 to 48 hours. Depending on your juicer and juicing conditions, you may be able to store a juice for up to 72 hours. Check with the manufacturer for its recommendations.

Fresh is best, but if you must store your juice, follow these guidelines:

- Oxygen is the enemy. You can use canning jars with a lid and a screw band and either fill the jar to the rim or use a vacuum sealer to remove the air.

- Store your juice in the coldest part of your refrigerator. You can also place your filled juice jars in the freezer for 10 to 15 mins to speed the cooling process before transferring them to the refrigerator. (Set a timer so you don't forget about them!)

- Add some lemon or lime to your juice blend to help maintain the freshness of your juice.

Losing Weight Juices

There are many reasons why juicing is helpful in promoting weight loss. For one thing, replacing typical meals of processed or fast foods with freshly squeezed juice will not only provide an increase in nutrient content, but it will also offer a significant reduction in calories. The basic science of weight loss is this: if you burn more calories than you consume, you will lose weight. This doesn't mean that you have to spend two hours on the treadmill every day just to burn off the food you eat. Remember that your body burns calories throughout the day just by keeping your heart pumping and your other organs functioning.

Unfortunately, many individuals in Western culture take in way too many calories on a daily basis: much more than their bodies need to function. This results in excess calories that are not immediately needed being converted to fat and stored. If a majority of those excess calories are derived from processed or fast foods, the toxins from those foods will also be stored along with the new fat cells. Over time, your body becomes literally weighed down, and your organs may not function as well as they once did. This can lead to more weight gain, making it a self-perpetuating cycle.

To shed off extra pounds, it's crucial to maintain a calorie deficit to prompt your body to use up stored fat for energy. However, don't mistake this as a cue to limit your daily calorie intake to a few hundred calories only. Although you might experience swift weight loss through this approach, it's neither healthy nor sustainable.

If you juice as a component of a healthy diet, it could assist you to drop weight by boosting the amount of nutrients you're taking in, promoting the expulsion of excessive toxins out of your body, and assisting you in creating a calorie shortfall. All of these benefits come from the fact that juicing encourages the flushing of excessive toxins out of your body. You can begin regaining the healthy function of your organs once you switch from consuming unhealthful foods that are high in toxins to juices that are rich in nutrients. As soon as your body stops being subjected to an excessive amount of inbound toxins, it will be able to start getting free of the poisons it has collected.

Juicing for weight loss is beneficial for a number of reasons, one of which is that the juice made from fruits and vegetables contains natural appetite suppressants. You ought to be happy to read that the solution is far simpler compared to you might've imagined it would be if you have either heard concerning the unpleasant side effects connected with commercial appetite suppressants or if you have tested them yourself. Due to the high concentrations of dietary fiber and other nutrients that fruits and vegetables contain, eating them can help you feel fuller for longer and suppress food cravings. You will have a much easier time sticking to your diet plan and achieving the desired amount of weight reduction if you aren't forced to battle the sensation of hunger throughout the day.

VERY GREEN JUICE

Difficulty: ★★☆☆☆

Preparation time: 5 minutes

Servings: 1

Ingredients:

- 1/2 large cucumber
- 4 cups spinach
- 2 sticks celery
- 1/4 cup watercress
- 2 ½ cups Romaine lettuce
- 1/2 medium zucchini
- 1/2 lemon
- A tweak of salt (optional)

Directions:

1. Wash the entire vegetables. Chop cucumber into chunks. Cut celery into 2-inch pieces
2. Chop the zucchini into chunks. Tear the greens, and peel and halve the lemon.
3. Cut celery into 2-inch pieces. Peel the lemon and cut it into 2 halves.
4. Place cucumber, spinach, celery, watercress, lettuce, and lemon in the juicer and extract the juice.
5. Put into glasses and serve with ice.

ORANGE WEIGHT LOSS JUICE

Difficulty: ★★☆☆☆

Preparation time: 4 minutes

Servings: 1

Ingredients:

- 1 orange
- 1/2 lemon
- 2 carrots
- 1 inches of fresh ginger

Directions:

1. Wash the oranges, lemon, carrots, and ginger.
2. Peel the oranges and lemon. Separate them into segments.
3. Trim the carrots and chop them into chunks.
4. Place oranges, lemons, carrots, and ginger in a juicer and extract the juice.
5. Pour into glasses. Add some ice if desired.
6. Serve.

BEETROOT JUICE

Difficulty: ★★☆☆☆

Preparation time: 5 minutes

Servings: 1

Ingredients:

- 2 carrots
- 1 apple
- 1/4 cup mint leaves
- 1/2 beetroot
- 1/2 teaspoon lemon juice
- 1/2-inch piece of fresh ginger
- 3/4 glasses of water

Directions:

1. Wash all the vegetables. Trim the beetroot and carrots. Peel them if desired and chop them into chunks.
2. Core the apples and peel them if desired. Chop into chunks.
3. Peel ginger and cut it into slices.
4. Place ginger, mint, carrots, apples, beetroot, water, and lemon juice into a mixer and mix till uniform.
5. You can serve this way or strain and serve. Alternatively, blend the vegetables and apples with the peel on and strain after blending.

CABBAGE GREEN JUICE

Difficulty: ★★☆☆☆

Preparation time: 5 minutes

Servings: 1

Ingredients:

- 2 cups shredded cabbage
- 1-2 chard leaves
- 1 sticks celery
- 1 big green apple
- 1 cup sliced kale
- Juice of a small lemon

Directions:

1. Wash the apples and all the vegetables. Tear the chard into bite-size parts
2. Slice the celery into two-inch parts
3. Core the apples and chop them into chunks.
4. Place cabbage, chard, celery, kale, and apples in a juicer and extract the juice.
5. Include lemon juice & mix.
6. Put into glasses & serve.

SUPERFOOD JUICE

Difficulty: ★★★☆☆

Preparation time: 5 minutes

Servings: 1

Ingredients:

- 4 sweet apples
- 2 inches of fresh ginger
- 16 - 20 kale leaves
- 1 lemon

Directions:

1. Wash the apples, ginger, and kale leaves.

2. Core the apples and peel them if desired. Chop into chunks.

3. Peel the lemon and cut it into 2 halves.

4. Tear the kale leaves into bite-size pieces.

5. Place a few of the apple slices in the juicer. Next, add some of the kale leaves. Repeat this process until all the apple slices and kale leaves are juiced. Finally, add lemon halves. Once the juice is extracted, put it into a glass and serve.

LIMEY WEIGHT LOSS MIX

Difficulty: ★★☆☆☆

Preparation time: 3 minutes

Servings: 1

Ingredients:

- 2 pink grapefruits
- 1 lime

Directions:

1. Using a juicer or a citrus press, juice the grapefruits and lime.

2. Pour into a glass over ice and drink immediately.

FRUITY WEIGHT LOSS MIXED JUICE

Difficulty: ★★☆☆☆

Preparation time: 5 minutes

Servings: 1

Ingredients:

- 4 rounds pineapple
- 1 grapefruit (juice of one grapefruit)
- 1 cup water

Directions:

1. Skin the pineapple & slice into rounds.

2. Run through a juicer along with the grapefruit. Pour the juice into a tall glass, add 1 cup of water, stir well and drink immediately.

PRUNE JUICE

Difficulty: ★☆☆☆☆

Preparation time: 1 minute + soaking time

Servings: 1

Ingredients:

- 6 prunes
- 1 tsp. honey
- 1 tbsp. lemon juice

Directions:

1. Soak prunes in about ½ cup of water for 30 mins.
2. Add prunes and soaked water into a mixer. Mix till uniform.
3. Put into a glass. Add honey & lemon juice and stir.
4. Chill for an hour and serve.

TROPICAL JUICE

Difficulty: ★★☆☆☆

Preparation time: 5 minutes

Servings: 1

Ingredients:

- 1 cup fresh pineapple chunk
- 1/2 cup coconut water
- 1 inches of fresh ginger

Directions:

1. Peel the ginger then cut it into slices. Place pineapple and ginger in a mixer and mix till uniform.

2. Pour the juice into a jug or container. Include coconut water & stir.

3. Put into glasses and serve.

MINTY FAT BURNING JUICE

Difficulty: ★★☆☆☆

Preparation time: 4 minutes

Servings: 1

Ingredients:

- 1 pink grapefruit
- 2 oranges
- 1 bunch mint
- 1 head romaine lettuce

Directions:

1. Remove the skin of oranges & grapefruit.
2. Pass the citruses through a juicer along with mint & lettuce & relish.

SIMPLE BROCCOLI WEIGHT LOSS JUICE

Difficulty: ★★☆☆☆

Preparation time: 5 minutes

Servings: 1

Ingredients:

- 2 large broccolis (raw)
- 2 celery stalks
- 1 apple
- 1 lemon

Directions:

1. Place the whole broccoli in the juicer and juice it. The white pith should be left on the lemon.

2. Put in the other ingredients and juice until smooth. Serve in a tall glass.

3. Enjoy!

GRAPY WEIGHT LOSS JUICE

Difficulty: ★★☆☆☆

Preparation time: 4 minutes

Servings: 1

Ingredients:

- 1 ruby grapefruit
- 1 orange
- 2 carrots
- 1/2-inch portion of ginger

Directions:

1. Rinse and peel the entire ingredients.
2. Pass through a juicer
3. Drink immediately.

CARROT CITRUS JUICE

Difficulty: ★★☆☆☆

Preparation time: 5 minutes

Servings: 1

Ingredients:

- 1 carrots

- 1 inches of fresh ginger

- 2 oranges

- 1 lemon

Directions:

1. Wash the carrots, ginger, oranges, and lemons.

2. Trim the carrots and peel them if desired. Slice the ginger.

3. Peel the oranges then separate them into segments.

4. Place carrots, ginger, oranges, and lemons in the juicer and extract the juice.

5. Pour into 1 glass. Add crushed ice and serve.

Antiaging Juices

As we age, our bodies undergo numerous changes. One of the most apparent signs of aging is the deterioration of our skin's quality, resulting in fine lines, wrinkles, and age spots. However, the good news is that the aging process can be slowed down by consuming healthy and nutritious foods, including anti-aging juices.

Anti-aging juices are not only delicious but are also packed with essential vitamins and minerals that help to keep our bodies healthy and rejuvenated. These juices are rich in antioxidants, which help to fight off the free radicals that damage our cells, causing premature aging.

One of the most crucial benefits of anti-aging juices is that they are incredibly beneficial for our skin. The vitamins and minerals present in these juices help to promote collagen production, which is essential for maintaining our skin's elasticity. As we age, our body's capability to generate collagen reduces, and collagen, a protein that imparts firmness and elasticity to our skin, gets affected.

By incorporating anti-aging juices into our daily diet, we can help to boost our body's collagen production, leading to firmer and more youthful-looking skin. These juices are also packed with Vitamin C, which helps to protect our skin from UV damage, another leading cause of premature aging.

In addition to their benefits for our skin, anti-aging juices are also great for promoting overall health and well-being. They can help to boost our immune system, which becomes weaker as we age, making us more susceptible to illnesses and diseases.

The antioxidants present in anti-aging juices can also help to reduce inflammation in our bodies, which is another factor that contributes to aging. Inflammation is linked to several age-related conditions, including arthritis, heart disease, and Alzheimer's disease.

Some of the most popular anti-aging juices include pomegranate juice, blueberry juice, and green tea. Pomegranate juice is rich in antioxidants and has been shown to have anti-inflammatory properties, making it an excellent choice for those looking to slow down the aging process.

Anti-aging juices are an excellent way to promote overall health and well-being while slowing down the aging process. By incorporating these juices into our daily diet, we can help to protect our skin from premature aging, boost our immune system, and reduce the risk of age-related conditions. So, whether you prefer pomegranate juice, blueberry juice, or green tea, there is an anti-aging juice out there that can help you look and feel your best.

RED CABBAGE JUICE

Difficulty: ★★☆☆☆

Preparation time: 5 minutes

Servings: 1

Ingredients:

- 1 cup raspberries
- 2 cups shredded red cabbage
- 1 zucchini
- 2 large purple carrots (or sweet potatoes)

Directions:

1. Wash all the vegetables and plums or raspberries. Pit the plums if using.
2. Trim the zucchini and carrots and chop them into chunks. Cut the zucchini into about 2-inch pieces. Peel the sweet potatoes if using and chop them into chunks.
3. Place carrots or sweet potato, red cabbage, plums, and zucchini in the juicer and extract the juice. You can also put them all inside a mixer and mix till uniform. Strain the juice if you are blending them in a blender.
4. Put into a glass and serve.

ANTI-AGING CITRUS JUICE

Difficulty: ★★☆☆☆

Preparation time: 6 minutes

Servings: 1

Ingredients:

- 2 ½ mandarin oranges
- 1/4 grapefruit
- 1/4 lime
- 1/4 lemon
- 1 ½ oranges
- Agave syrup to taste (optional)

Directions:

1. Wash all the fruit. Cut them into 2 halves horizontally.

2. Squeeze the juice of all the citrus fruit on a citrus juicer.

3. You can also peel the citrus fruit and separate them into segments. Place them in a juicer and extract the juice. Blending them in a blender can make the juice bitter, as the seeds will get ground. It is better to avoid making this juice in a blender.

4. Stir well and pour into glasses. Add agave nectar to taste if desired.

5. Add ice and serve.

POMEGRANATE AND MINT JUICE

Difficulty: ★★☆☆☆

Preparation time: 5 minutes

Servings: 1

Ingredients:

- 1/2 cup packed mint leaves
- 1 pomegranates

Directions:

1. Wash the pomegranates and cut them open. Remove the seeds. Use the seeds to make juice.

2. Place pomegranate seeds and mint leaves in a blender. Give short pulses until you can see juice. The seeds should not be ground. But then some seeds may be broken a bit while pulsing.

3. Pour the juice into a strainer and strain the juice.

4. Pour the juice into 1 glass. Garnish with some mint leaves and serve.

ZUCCHINI JUICE

Difficulty: ★★★☆☆

Preparation time: 5 minutes

Servings: 1

Ingredients:

- 1 cup cherries
- 2 sweet potatoes
- 1 zucchini
- 2 large purple carrots

Directions:

1. Wash all the vegetables and cherries. Pit the cherries.

2. Trim the zucchini and carrots and chop them into chunks. Cut the zucchini into about 2-inch pieces. Peel the sweet potatoes if desired and chop them into chunks.

3. Place carrots, sweet potato, cherries, and zucchini in the juicer and extract the juice. You can also put them all inside a mixer and mix till uniform. Strain the juice if you are blending them in a blender.

4. Put into a glass and serve.

SKIN CARE CELERY JUICE

Difficulty: ★★☆☆☆

Preparation time: 4 minutes

Servings: 1

Ingredients:

- 1 cup celery leaves
- 1 tsp. lemon juice
- 1/2 cup of water
- 1/2 medium cucumber
- 1 heaped tablespoon seaweed flakes

Directions:

1. Wash celery and cucumber. Chop cucumber into chunks.
2. Place celery, lemon juice, water, cucumber, and seaweed flakes inside a mixer & mix till uniform.
3. Put into a glass & present.

CUCUMBER AND LIME JUICE

Difficulty: ★★☆☆☆

Preparation time: 3 minutes

Servings: 1

Ingredients:

- 1 cucumber
- 1/4 cup water
- 1 teaspoon lime juice or to taste
- Ice cubes, as required

Directions:

1. Wash the cucumber. Peel the cucumber and chop it into chunks.

2. Add water & mix till uniform. Put the juice into a strainer and strain the juice.

3. Pour the juice into a glass. Add lime juice and stir.

4. Add ice cubes and serve.

CUCUMBER JUICE

Difficulty: ★☆☆☆☆

Preparation time: 5 minutes

Servings: 1

Ingredients:

- 1/2 cucumber
- 1 apple
- 2 medium carrots
- 1/2 celery stalk

Directions:

1. Wash the vegetables and apple. Core the apple, peel if desired, and chop it into chunks.

2. Chop cucumber into chunks. Trim the carrots and cut them into pieces.

3. Cut the celery into slices. Place cucumber, celery, apple, and carrots in a blender and blender and blend until smooth.

BEET GRAPE JUICE

Difficulty: ★★☆☆☆

Preparation time: 4 minutes

Servings: 1

Ingredients:

- 1 cup red grapes
- 2 beetroots
- 2 sticks celery
- 2 large carrots

Directions:

1. Wash all the vegetables and grapes. Use the beet greens if you like them. It's very healthy.

2. Trim the beetroots and carrots and chop them into chunks. Cut the celery into about 2-inch pieces.

3. Place carrots, beetroots, grapes, and celery in the juicer and extract the juice. You can also put them all inside a mixer and mix till uniform. Strain the juice if you are blending them in a blender.

4. Put into a glass and serve with ice.

Antiaging Juices

APPLE AND BEETROOT JUICE

Difficulty: ★★☆☆☆

Preparation time: 5 minutes

Servings: 1

Ingredients:

- 1/2 beetroot
- 1 Fuji apples
- 1/2-inch fresh ginger
- 5 lettuce leaves
- Lemon juice (or more, as required)

Directions:

1. Rinse the beetroot, apples, ginger, and lettuce.

2. Core the apples and chop them into chunks. Trim the beets and chop them into chunks.

3. Peel ginger and cut it into slices.

4. Place the beetroot, lettuce, ginger, and apples in a juicer in the order mentioned.

5. You can also put them all inside a mixer and mix till uniform. Strain the juice if you are blending them in a blender.

6. Extract the juice and add lemon juice.

7. Pour into glasses and serve with ice if desired.

FRESH START

Difficulty: ★★☆☆☆

Preparation time: 6 minutes

Servings: 1

Ingredients:

- 1 small cucumber
- 1 small bunch of cilantros, with leaves and stems
- 1 small bunch of parsley, with leaves and stems
- 2 kale leaves
- 1 tbsp. fresh lime juice
- 1/2 large green apple

Directions:

1. Wash all the greens, the apple, and the cucumber.
2. Core the apple and chop it into chunks
3. Chop the cucumbers into chunks. Chop the parsley and cilantro. Tear the kale leaves
4. Place the cucumber, apple, and greens in the juicer and extract the juice. You can also put them all inside a mixer and mix till uniform. Strain the juice if you are blending them in a blender.
5. Include lime juice & mix.
6. Put into a glass & serve.

GLOWING SKIN JUICE

Difficulty: ★★☆☆☆

Preparation time: 4 minutes

Servings: 1

Ingredients:

- 1/2 apple
- 1/2 cup pineapple chunks
- 1/2 cucumber
- 1 cup of water

Directions:

1. Wash the apple and cucumber.
2. Core the apple. Peel the apple if desired and chop it into chunks. Peel the cucumber if desired and chop it into chunks.
3. Blend apple, cucumber, pineapple, and water in a blender until smooth. Strain if desired.
4. Pour into 1 glass. Serve with ice if desired.

CARROT AND LEMON JUICE

Difficulty: ★★☆☆☆

Preparation time: 5 minutes

Servings: 1

Ingredients:

- 1 tbsp. fresh lemon juice
- 6-8 medium carrots

Directions:

1. Trim the carrots and chop them into chunks.

2. Place the carrots in the juicer and extract the juice.

3. Put into a glass. Include lemon juice and mix. Add some crushed ice or ice cubes and serve.

ANTI-AGING ALOE JUICE

Difficulty: ★★☆☆☆

Preparation time: 6 minutes

Servings: 1

Ingredients:

- 1 small cucumbers
- 1/4 cup blueberries
- Lime juice
- 1/8 cup fresh Aloe Vera gel
- 1-inch fresh ginger, cut
- 1/4 cup chopped red bell peppers
- A handful spinach

Directions:

1. Wash the cucumbers, blueberries, bell peppers, spinach, and ginger. Chop cucumber and ginger into pieces, and tear the spinach leaves.

2. Take a piece of leaf from an aloe Vera leaf. Remove the thick green part of the leaf and measure out 1/4 cup of the gel.

3. Add cucumber, spinach, ginger, blueberries, red bell pepper, and aloe Vera gel inside a mixer. Mix till uniform.

4. Strain the juice. Add lime juice and stir.

5. Pour into the glass.

6. Serve with ice cubes.

Detoxifying and Cleansing Juices

If you are familiar with the juicing trend, you may have also heard of a juice cleanse. Also known as a juice fast, it involves consuming nothing but fruit and vegetable juices for a predetermined length of time. Though long-term fasting of this kind is generally not recommended, a three- to five-day juice cleanse may provide numerous health benefits. Skeptics of juice cleansing suggest that there is no scientific evidence to support the idea that consuming fresh fruit and vegetable juices will rid your body of toxins. While juicing may not be a magical solution to the world's health problems, it does provide a number of benefits that may help to cleanse and detoxify your body.

The modern Western diet is centered on processed foods, which are loaded with artificial preservatives, flavors, and other toxins. Thankfully, the human body is designed to filter out and eliminate these toxins; however, the average Western diet creates a toxic load much higher than the body is capable of handling. Your liver, kidneys, lungs, and skin are the primary detoxifying organs in your body, and when they become overloaded, your body may begin storing excess toxins in your fat cells and tissues. Over time, your body will become toxic and you may experience a number of negative side effects, including indigestion, allergies, constipation, dry hair and skin, breakouts, and more.

It is important to understand that fresh fruit and vegetable juices will not magically make the toxins in your body disappear. Juicing can, however, play a role in naturally detoxifying your body. Engaging in a juice cleanse means that you will stop poisoning your body with toxic-laden processed foods, replacing them instead with nutrient-rich juices. If, after you complete your juice cleanse, you continue to avoid processed foods and maintain a habit of consuming fresh fruits and vegetables, your body will naturally begin to recover from its toxic overload. By reducing your intake of toxins, your body will be able to focus on stored toxins and flush them from your system, which will result in improved overall health.

WATERMELON DETOX

Difficulty: ★☆☆☆☆

Preparation time: 5 minutes

Servings: 1

Ingredients:

- 1 cup watermelon chunks
- 2-3 tablespoons fresh lime juice
- 1/2 cup strawberries
- 1/2-inch piece of fresh ginger

Directions:

1. Peel and cut a fresh watermelon and chop them into chunks. Remove the seeds, if any. Measure out 1 cup of watermelon chunks.
2. Hull the strawberries and cut them into 2 halves. Peel the ginger then cut it into thin slices.
3. Place watermelon, lime juice, and strawberries inside a mixer & mix till uniform.
4. Include some ice & mix till uniform.
5. Put into glasses and serve.

LIVER DETOXIFIER

Difficulty: ★★☆☆☆

Preparation time: 5 minutes

Servings: 1

Ingredients:

- half beetroot
- 2 carrots
- 1/2 bunch spinach
- Lemon juice
- 1/2 small bunch of parsley
- 1/2 cucumber
- 3 celery sticks

Directions:

1. Wash all the vegetables.
2. Trim the beetroot and carrots and chop them into chunks.
3. Chop cucumber and celery into pieces. Tear the spinach and parsley.
4. Place beets, carrots, spinach, parsley, cucumber, and celery in a juicer and extract the juice.
5. Put into glasses & offer.

KALE AND PEAR JUICE

Difficulty: ★★☆☆☆

Preparation time: 4 minutes

Servings: 1

Ingredients:

- 2 kale leaves
- 1/2 lime
- 3 large sticks of celery
- 1 cups spinach
- 1 medium pear
- Ice cubes (as required)

Directions:

1. Wash all the greens, pears, and lime.

2. Peel the lime. Chop the spinach, kale, and celery. Core the pears and cut them into wedges.

3. First, place the pear wedges into the juicer. Next, add in the greens and lime and extract the juice. You can also put them all inside a mixer and mix till uniform. Strain the juice if you are blending them in a blender.

4. Pour into 1 glass. Add ice cubes and serve.

Detoxifying and Cleaning Juices

LETTUCE AND APPLE JUICE

Difficulty: ★☆☆☆☆

Preparation time: 5 minutes

Servings: 1

Ingredients:

- 1 green apple
- 1/2 cucumber
- 1 tbsp. fresh lemon juice (or as required)
- 3 sticks of celery without leaves
- 2 cups lettuce leaves

Directions:

1. Wash the apple and vegetables.
2. Core the apples and slice them into wedges. Chop the cucumbers into chunks. Cut the celery into 2-inch pieces, and tear up the lettuce leaves.
3. Place the apples, cucumber, celery, and lettuce in the juicer and extract the juice. You can also put them all inside a mixer and mix till uniform. Strain the juice if you are blending them in a blender.
4. Add lemon juice and stir.
5. Put into a glass & offer.

GREEN JUICE WITH PEARS

Difficulty: ★★☆☆☆

Preparation time: 5 minutes

Servings: 1

Ingredients:

- 1/4 cup fresh parsley
- 1/4 lemon
- 3 large sticks of celery
- 1 ½ cups spinach
- 1 medium pear
- Ice cubes, as required

Directions:

1. Wash all the greens, pear, and lemon.
2. Peel the lemon. Chop the spinach, parsley, and celery. Core the pears and cut them into wedges.
3. First, place the pear wedges in the juicer. Next, add the greens and lemon and extract the juice.
4. Pour into a glass. Add ice cubes & offer.

Detoxifying and Cleaning Juices

SUMMER JUICE

Difficulty: ★☆☆☆☆

Preparation time: 5 minutes

Servings: 1

Ingredients:

- 1 cup chopped fresh pineapple chunks
- 2 carrots
- 1/2-inch piece of ginger
- 1/2 lemon
- 2 sticks of celery

Directions:

1. Rinse the fresh pineapple and vegetables.

2. Skin a fresh pineapple and chop it into chunks. Measure out 1 cup of pineapple. Use the remaining for the next day or eat it as a snack.

3. Trim the carrots and chop them into chunks. Slice the celery into pieces.

4. Peel and slice the ginger. Peel the lemon.

5. Juice pineapple, carrots, celery, ginger, and lemon in a juicer.

6. You can also put them all inside a mixer & mix till uniform. Strain the juice if you are blending them in a blender.

7. Pour into 1 glass and serve.

LET'S BEET IT

Difficulty: ★★☆☆☆

Preparation time: 4 minutes

Servings: 1

Ingredients:

- 1 beet
- 4 kale leaves
- 4 sticks celery
- 1 cucumber
- Juice of 1 lemon

Directions:

1. Wash all the vegetables. Chop beets and cucumber into chunks.

2. Tear up the kale leaves. Chop celery into pieces.

3. Place the cucumber, celery, and kale in the juicer and extract the juice. You can also put them all inside a mixer & mix till uniform. Strain the juice if you are blending them in a blender.

4. Include lemon juice & mix.

5. Put into 1 glass & serve.

GREEN DETOX JUICE

Difficulty: ★★☆☆☆

Preparation time: 5 minutes

Servings: 1

Ingredients:

- 1/2 green apple
- 1/2 large English cucumber
- 1 tbsp. fresh lemon juice
- 1 large handful of parsley with stems and leaves
- 1 cup packed baby spinach
- 1/2 inch fresh ginger

Directions:

1. Wash the apple & vegetables.
2. Core the apples and slice them into wedges. Chop the cucumbers into chunks. Cut the parsley into parts.
3. Place apples, cucumber, spinach, parsley, and ginger in the juicer and extract the juice. You can also put them all inside a mixer & mix till uniform. Strain the juice if you are blending them in a blender.
4. Include lemon juice & mix.
5. Put into a glass & serve.

THE SUPER DETOXER

Difficulty: ★★☆☆☆

Preparation time: 6 minutes

Servings: 1

Ingredients:

- 1 cucumber
- 1 small bunch of cilantros, with leaves and stems
- 1 small bunch of parsley, with leaves and stems
- 2 kale leaves
- 2 tablespoons fresh lemon juice or to taste
- 4 sticks celery
- 2 Swiss chard leaves
- A pinch of cayenne pepper (optional)
- 2 inches of fresh ginger

Directions:

1. Rinse all the green vegetables as well as the cucumber.
2. Slice the cucumbers into chunks. Cut the celery into 2-inch pieces, and tear up the greens. Peel the ginger then cut it into slices.
3. Place the cucumber, celery, and greens in the juicer and extract the juice. You can also put them all inside a mixer and mix till uniform. Strain the juice if you are blending them in a blender.
4. Add lemon juice and cayenne pepper and stir.
5. Put into a glass and serve.

CILANTRO WITH PEAR DETOX DELIGHT

Difficulty: ★★☆☆☆

Preparation time: 5 minutes

Servings: 1

Ingredients:

- 1 medium zucchini
- 1 firm pear
- Handful cilantro
- 1/2 large cucumber

Directions:

1. To prepare the items, you may want to skin, slice, de-seed, or mince them.
2. Put a bowl just below the outlet of the juicer.
3. Put all of the components into the juicer in the sequence that they are catalogued.
4. Alternate ingredients, finishing with the cucumber.
5. Stir the juice and pour into glasses to serve.

HEALTHY DETOX JUICE

Difficulty: ★★☆☆☆

Preparation time: 5 minutes

Servings: 1

Ingredients:

- 1 green apple
- 1/2 cucumber
- 1 tbsp. fresh lemon juice
- 2 sticks celery
- 3 kale leaves
- 1/2 inch fresh ginger

Directions:

1. Wash the apple and vegetables.
2. Core the apple and cut it into wedges. Chop the cucumbers into chunks. Cut the celery into 2-inch pieces, and tear up the kale leaves.
3. Place the apples, cucumber, kale, celery, and ginger in the juicer and extract the juice. You can also put them all inside a mixer and mix till uniform. Strain the juice if you are blending them in a blender.
4. Include lemon juice & mix.
5. Put into a glass & offer.

BEET, CARROT AND GINGER JUICE

Difficulty: ★★☆☆☆

Preparation time: 4 minutes

Servings: 1

Ingredients:

- 1/2 inch fresh ginger
- 2 carrots
- 2 beets
- 2 sticks celery

Directions:

1. Wash the vegetables and chop them into chunks. Peel the ginger then cut it into slices. Cut the celery into pieces. Trim the carrots and beets and chop them into chunks.
2. Place beets, carrots, ginger, and celery in the juicer and extract the juice. You can also put them all inside a mixer & mix till uniform. Strain the juice if you are blending them in a blender.
3. Pour into a glass and serve with crushed ice.

TROPICAL MINTY JUICE

Difficulty: ★★☆☆☆

Preparation time: 5 minutes

Servings: 1

Ingredients:

- 2 sticks celery
- 2 cups spinach
- 1 cup fresh pineapple chunks
- 1/2 cucumber
- 2 ½ cups fresh mint leaves

Directions:

1. Wash the fresh pineapple and vegetables.
2. Peel a fresh pineapple and chop it into chunks. Measure out 1 cup of pineapple. Use the remaining for the next day or eat it as a snack.
3. Tear the spinach into large pieces. Chop cucumber into chunks, and cut the celery into about 2-inch pieces.
4. Place celery, spinach, mint, pineapple, and cucumber in the order mentioned in the juicer, i.e., first place celery followed by spinach, etc. Extract the juice.
5. Pour into 1 glass and offer alongside ice.

Energizing Juices

Juices have been a part of human nutrition for centuries. As people have become more health-conscious, they have sought out juices that can energize and revitalize their bodies. Energizing juices are a popular choice for those looking to increase their energy levels, improve their digestion, and boost their immune systems. These juices are made from a combination of fruits and vegetables that are rich in vitamins, minerals, and other nutrients that can help to increase energy and promote overall wellness.

The benefits of energizing juices are numerous. First and foremost, they can help to increase energy levels. Many people experience a mid-day slump or feel tired and sluggish in the morning. Drinking an energizing juice can help to provide a quick burst of energy that can help to power through the day. These juices are also a great way to improve digestion. The combination of fruits and vegetables in these juices can help to promote healthy digestion and relieve constipation.

In addition to increasing energy levels and improving digestion, energizing juices can also help to boost the immune system. The high levels of vitamins and minerals in these juices can help to strengthen the immune system and ward off illness. These juices are also a great way to detoxify the body. The combination of fruits and vegetables in these juices can help to flush toxins from the body, which can help to improve overall health and wellbeing.

Vegetables and fruit juices are rich sources of electrolytes like magnesium, potassium, calcium, and sodium, electrolytes important for metabolism, stabilizing blood sugar levels, and for proper muscles and brain functioning. As these changes occur in your body, you become more energetic.

Moreover, juices are also rich in vitamins A, B and C, vitamins that boost your mental and physical energy. Further, juices are directly absorbed into your bloodstream; this means your body takes them up very fast since the body does not have to digest them before utilizing them. This means that as you drink a juice, you get an instant energy boost.

Energizing juices are a great way to increase energy levels, improve digestion, boost the immune system, and promote overall wellness. Whether you prefer green juice, citrus juice, or another type of juice, these beverages are an easy and convenient way to get the nutrients that your body needs to function at its best. With so many different types of energizing juices available, it is easy to find a recipe that suits your tastes and meets your nutritional needs. So why not try making an energizing juice today and see how it can benefit your health and wellbeing?

CARROT APPLE ZINGER

Difficulty: ★★☆☆☆

Preparation time: 5 minutes

Servings: 1

Ingredients:

- 1 apple
- 1/2 lemon
- 2 carrots
- 1-inch piece of fresh ginger

Directions:

1. Rinse the apple, carrots, lemon, and ginger.
2. Peel ginger and cut it into slices. Peel the lemon and cut it into pieces.
3. Peel the carrots if desired and chop them into chunks.
4. Core the apples then slice them into portions.
5. Place apples, carrots, lemon, and ginger in the juicer and extract the juice. You can also add the components into a mixer and mix till uniform but ensure to strain the juice before serving.
6. Pour into a glass. Serve with ice.

CHARD WITH KALE PROTEIN POWER

Difficulty: ★★★☆☆

Preparation time: 5 minutes

Servings: 1

Ingredients:

- 1 cup pineapple
- 5 kale leaves
- 3 chard leaves
- 1 cucumber
- 2 scoops plant-based protein powder

Directions:

1. Wash the kale, chard, and cucumber.
2. Trim the ends and skin from the pineapple, then remove the core and discard. Slice pineapple into one-inch chunks.
3. Clip the ends from the cucumber, afterwards slice into 4-inch pieces.
4. Put a pitcher below the juicer's spout to collect the juice.
5. Feed the first four ingredients through the juicer's intake tube in the order listed.
6. When the juice stops flowing, remove the pitcher, add the protein powder, and stir.
7. Serve immediately.

ORANGE JUICE

Difficulty: ★☆☆☆☆

Preparation time: 5 minutes

Servings: 1

Ingredients:

- 1 orange
- 1 carrot
- 1/2 red apple

Directions:

1. Wash oranges, carrots, and the apple.

2. Peel the oranges then separate them into segments.

3. Core the apple and cut it into pieces.

4. Trim the carrots and chop them into chunks.

5. Place oranges, carrots, and the apple in the juicer and extract the juice.

6. You can also blend them all in a blender until smooth, but you need to strain the juice.

7. Pour into glasses and serve with ice.

APPLE BERRY JUICE

Difficulty: ★★☆☆☆

Preparation time: 5 minutes

Servings: 1

Ingredients:

- 2 green apples
- 1 red apples
- 2 cups fresh raspberries

Directions:

1. Wash the fruit. Core the apples and slice them into portions.
2. Put half the apples and raspberries in the juicer and extract the juice. Add remaining apples and extract the juice.
3. Put into glasses and serve with crushed ice.

WATERMELON KIWI

Difficulty: ★★☆☆☆

Preparation time: 4 minutes

Servings: 1

Ingredients:

- 1 ½ cups watermelon chunks
- Juice of one lime
- 2 kiwis

Directions:

1. Wash the kiwis. Peel them and chop them into chunks. Remove the seeds from the watermelon.

2. Add watermelon, lime juice, and kiwis into a mixer & mix till very uniform.

3. Put into 1 glass. Add crushed ice & serve.

KIWI GREEN APPLE SPINACH

Difficulty: ★★☆☆☆

Preparation time: 5 minutes

Servings: 1

Ingredients:

- 2 apples
- 2 kiwis
- 1 cups spinach

Directions:

1. Wash the fruit and spinach.
2. Tear the spinach into pieces. Core the apples and slice them into portions.
3. Skin the kiwis and chop them into chunks.
4. Place a few kiwi chunks in the juicer, followed by spinach. Place remaining kiwi and extract the juice.
5. Next, add apples and extract the juice.
6. Pour into glasses and serve with crushed ice.
7. Pour into glasses. Serve with ice.

SUNRISE SURPRISE

Difficulty: ★★☆☆☆

Preparation time: 4 minutes

Servings: 1

Ingredients:

- 1/2 lime
- 1 cup fresh pineapple cubes
- 1/2 pound carrots

Directions:

1. Peel the lime half. Wash and chop the carrots into chunks.

2. Place pineapple, carrots, and lime in a juicer and extract the juice.

3. Put into a glass and serve with ice if anticipated.

PINEAPPLE SPINACH GINGER

Difficulty: ★★☆☆☆

Preparation time: 5 minutes

Servings: 1

Ingredients:

- 2 ½ cups chopped fresh pineapple
- 2 inches of fresh ginger
- 2 cups spinach

Directions:

1. Wash the spinach and ginger. Tear up the spinach leaves into pieces, and peel and slice the ginger.
2. First, add a few pieces of pineapple into the juicer, followed by spinach, ginger, and the remaining pineapple.
3. Extract the juice. Pour into glasses and serve with ice.

APPLE CITRUS

Difficulty: ★☆☆☆☆

Preparation time: 5 minutes

Servings: 1

Ingredients:

- 1 green apple
- 1/2 orange
- 1/2 grapefruit
- 1/2-inch piece of fresh ginger (optional)

Directions:

1. Wash the fruit and ginger if used.
2. Core the apples and chop them into portions.
3. Skin the orange and grapefruit and separate them into segments.
4. First, add grapefruit into the juicer and extract the juice. Next, add ginger, apple, and oranges and extract the juice.

GREEN MACHINE

Difficulty: ★★☆☆☆

Preparation time: 5 minutes

Servings: 1

Ingredients:

- 2 cups spinach
- 1 green apples
- 1 lemon
- 1 cucumber
- 2 inches of fresh ginger

Directions:

1. Wash the vegetables and apples.
2. Core the apples and chop them into portions. Skin the lemon and chop it into pieces.
3. Chop cucumber into chunks. Peel ginger and cut it into slices.
4. Place a few pieces of lemon in the juicer. Place spinach over the lemon and some more lemon over the spinach. Set the juicer on low speed and extract the juice.
5. Next, add cucumber and raise the speed to high speed. Add ginger and apples and extract the juice.

THE ENERGY BOOSTER

Difficulty: ★★☆☆☆

Preparation time: 5 minutes

Servings: 1

Ingredients:

- 1 ½ green apples
- 1/2 bunch spinach
- 1 sticks celery

Directions:

1. Wash the apples and vegetables. Core the apples and slice them into portions.
2. Slice celery into two-inch parts.
3. Tear the spinach into large pieces.
4. Place some apple pieces in the juicer. Next, add spinach, followed by celery, and finally the remaining apples.
5. Extract the juice. Pour into 1 glass and serve with ice.

ENERGETIC RAINBOW JUICE

Difficulty: ★★☆☆☆

Preparation time: 5 minutes

Servings: 1

Ingredients:

- 1/2 beet
- 1/2 orange
- A small handful of blueberries
- 1/2 carrot
- A small handful of spinach
- 1/4 inch of fresh ginger

Directions:

1. Wash all the fruit and vegetables well.
2. Peel the orange and separate the segments.
3. Peel the ginger then cut it into slices.
4. Trim the carrot and beetroot and cut them into pieces.
5. Place orange, carrot, beet, ginger, and blueberries in a juicer and extract the juice.
6. Pour into glasses and serve with ice.

BREAKFAST ZINGER JUICE

Difficulty: ★★☆☆☆

Preparation time: 4 minutes

Servings: 1

Ingredients:

- 1 apple
- 1 lemon
- 1 carrot
- 1 beet

Directions:

1. Wash the apple, carrots, lemon, and beet.
2. Peel the lemon and cut it into pieces.
3. Peel the carrot and beetroot if desired and chop them into chunks.
4. Core the apple then cut it into chunks.
5. Place apple, carrot, lemon, and beet in the juicer and extract the juice. You can also add the components into a mixer and mix till uniform but ensure to strain the juice before serving.
6. Put into a glass. Serve with ice.

Anti-Inflammatory Juices

When our immune system detects a threat, such as an injury, infection, or other noxious stimulus, it reacts in a normal way by triggering inflammation. While acute inflammation is necessary for the body to heal, chronic inflammation could lead to numerous health issues, like heart disease, arthritis, and even cancer. To combat chronic inflammation, many people turn to anti-inflammatory juices as a natural remedy.

Anti-inflammatory juices are made from fruits and vegetables that are rich in nutrients and antioxidants that can reduce inflammation in the body. These juices provide a quick and convenient way to get a concentrated dose of essential vitamins and minerals, which can help to alleviate chronic inflammation.

One of the key ingredients in anti-inflammatory juices is turmeric. Curcumin is a potent anti-inflammatory compound found in turmeric that has been demonstrated to reduce inflammation within the body. In addition to turmeric, anti-inflammatory juices often include other anti-inflammatory ingredients, such as ginger, spinach, kale, berries, and citrus fruits.

Ginger is another potent anti-inflammatory ingredient commonly found in anti-inflammatory juices. It contains gingerol, a compound that has been shown to reduce inflammation and pain. Ginger has been used for centuries in traditional medicine to treat a variety of ailments, including inflammation.

Spinach and kale are both nutrient-dense greens that are high in vitamins and antioxidants. These leafy greens are excellent sources of vitamin K, which is essential for healthy bones and blood clotting. They also contain high levels of vitamin A, which is crucial for eye health, and vitamin C, which is an antioxidant that can help to reduce inflammation.

Anti-inflammatory juices often include berries like blueberries, strawberries, and raspberries, as they are abundant in antioxidants like anthocyanins, which have anti-inflammatory properties and shield the cells against damage. Moreover, berries are an excellent fiber source that supports healthy digestion.

Citrus fruits like oranges, lemons, and grapefruits are abundant sources of antioxidants, including vitamin C, which can counteract free radicals and safeguard against cellular harm. Additionally, these fruits contain flavonoids, which are substances with demonstrated anti-inflammatory properties.

Consuming juices that have anti-inflammatory properties is an excellent approach to obtaining a concentrated amount of vital nutrients that can aid in diminishing inflammation within the body. These juices are made from fruits and vegetables that are rich in nutrients and antioxidants, such as turmeric, ginger, spinach, kale, berries, and citrus fruits. Incorporating anti-inflammatory juices into your diet may help to reduce inflammation and improve overall health. However, it is important to note that anti-inflammatory juices should not be used as a substitute for medical treatment and advice from a healthcare professional.

THE GREEN GRAPE JUICE

Difficulty: ★★☆☆☆

Preparation time: 5 minutes

Servings: 1

Ingredients:

- 1/4 lemon
- 1 cup grapes
- 1 inches fresh ginger
- 1 bunches kale

Directions:

1. Wash lemon, grapes, ginger, and kale.

2. Peel the lemon. Peel the ginger then cut it into slices. Tear the kale leaves.

3. Place lemon, grapes, ginger, and kale in a juicer and extract the juice.

4. Pour into 1 glass and serve.

APPLE AND FENNEL JUICE

Difficulty: ★★☆☆☆

Preparation time: 5 minutes

Servings: 1

Ingredients:

- 1 tbsp. lemon juice
- 1 large apple
- 1 cup mint leaves
- 1/2 fennel bulb
- 1/2 cucumber
- 2 cups spinach leaves

Directions:

1. Wash the vegetables and apple.
2. Core the apple and chop it into chunks. Chop fennel bulb and cucumber into smaller pieces.
3. Tear spinach leaves.
4. Place apple, mint, and spinach in a juicer. Extract the juice. Add fennel and cucumber and extract the juice.
5. Include lemon juice & mix.
6. Put into a glass & serve with ice cubes.

CHERRY MANGO JUICE

Difficulty: ★★☆☆☆

Preparation time: 4 minutes

Servings: 1

Ingredients:

- 3/4 cup sweet cherries
- 1/2 mango
- 1/2 cup water

Directions:

1. Wash the fruit. Pit the cherries. Peel and chop the mango.
2. Place cherries, mango, and water inside a mixer & mix till uniform.
3. Strain if desired and serve using ice.

GINGER TURMERIC CARROT SHOTS

Difficulty: ★★☆☆☆

Preparation time: 5 minutes

Servings: 1

Ingredients:

- 1/4 pound carrots
- 1/2 inch of fresh ginger
- A bit of salt
- 1/2 inch of fresh turmeric
- 3 to 4 tablespoons unsweetened coconut water

Directions:

1. Wash the vegetables.
2. Coarsely chop the carrots. Peel the ginger and turmeric and coarsely chop them as well.
3. Place ginger, turmeric, and carrots in a blender. Add half the coconut water & mix till uniform.
4. Strain the solution into a bowl. Include remaining coconut water and stir.
5. Add salt and stir. Serve in shot glasses.

MANGO CITRUS JUICE

Difficulty: ★★☆☆☆

Preparation time: 6 minutes

Servings: 1

Ingredients:

- 1/2 banana
- 1/2 mango
- 1 apple
- 1/4 lemon
- 1 orange
- 1 inch piece of fresh ginger

Directions:

1. Wash all the fruit, lemon, and ginger.
2. Peel the banana then cut it into pieces. Peel the mango and chop it into chunks.
3. Core the apple and cut it into wedges.
4. Peel the lemon. Peel the orange and separate the segments.
5. Peel and slice the ginger.
6. Place banana, mango, lemon, orange, ginger, and apple in a juicer and extract the juice.
7. You can also blend them all in a blender until smooth.
8. Strain the juice.
9. Pour into a glass.
10. Add ice and serve.

GOUT AND JOINT PAIN JUICE

Difficulty: ★★☆☆☆

Preparation time: 5 minutes

Servings: 1

Ingredients:

- 1 medium cucumbers
- 1/2 lemon
- 2 sticks celery
- 1 inches of fresh ginger

Directions:

1. Wash the vegetables.
2. Chop the cucumbers into chunks. Slice celery into two-inch parts.
3. Peel the lemon and ginger, and cut the ginger into slices.
4. Place cucumbers, lemon, celery, and ginger in the juicer and extract the juice.
5. Put into glasses and serve with ice.

CITRUS, TURMERIC, AND GINGER JUICE

Difficulty: ★★☆☆☆

Preparation time: 5 minutes

Servings: 1

Ingredients:

- 2 Fiji apples
- 1/2 lemon
- 1 inch of fresh turmeric or one tsp. turmeric powder
- 1 orange
- 1 inches of fresh ginger

Directions:

1. Wash the fruit, lemon, turmeric, and ginger.
2. Core and chop the apples. Peel the lemon and oranges.
3. Separate the orange segments. Peel ginger and turmeric and cut into slices.
4. Place apples, turmeric, ginger, lemon, and oranges in a juicer and extract the juice.
5. Pour into glasses. If using turmeric powder, add it now and stir.
6. Serve with ice.

PINEAPPLE, CUCUMBER, AND TURMERIC

Difficulty: ★★☆☆☆

Preparation time: 5 minutes

Servings: 1

Ingredients:

- 2 cups fresh pineapple pieces
- 3-4 pieces of fresh turmeric (3 inches each)
- 2 small cucumbers
- 1/4 tablespoon ground cinnamon

Directions:

1. Wash the turmeric and cucumbers. Peel the turmeric and chop it into chunks.
2. Place turmeric, pineapple, and cucumbers in a juicer and extract the juice. You can also blend the components inside a mixer till uniform.
3. Strain the juice if using a blender. Add cinnamon and stir.
4. Pour into glasses and serve with ice.

ANTI-INFLAMMATORY TONIC

Difficulty: ★★☆☆☆

Preparation time: 5 minutes

Servings: 1

Ingredients:

- 1 inch fresh turmeric
- 1/2 inch fresh ginger
- 1/2 lemon
- 4 carrots
- 1 orange
- 3 sticks celery

Directions:

1. Wash all the vegetables and oranges. Peel ginger and turmeric and cut into slices.
2. Peel the lemon and cut it into halves or quarters
3. Trim the carrots and chop them into chunks. Peel the oranges and separate the segments.
4. Cut celery into 2-inch pieces.
5. Place turmeric, ginger, lemon, carrots, oranges, and celery in a juicer.
6. Extract the juice. Pour into glasses and serve using crushed ice.

CARROT AND GINGER JUICE

Difficulty: ★★☆☆☆

Preparation time: 5 minutes

Servings: 1

Ingredients:

- 7 to 8 carrots
- 1 inch of fresh ginger
- 1 lemon

Directions:

1. Wash the vegetables. Trim the carrots and chop them into chunks
2. Peel the lemons and cut them into quarters.
3. Peel the ginger then cut it into slices.
4. Place carrots, ginger, and lemon in the juicer and extract the juice.
5. Pour the juice into glasses and serve with ice.

GINGER BEET JUICE

Difficulty: ★★☆☆☆

Preparation time: 5 minutes

Servings: 1

Ingredients:

- 2 oranges
- 2 apples
- 1/2 large beet + beet greens
- 6 kale leaves
- 1/2 carrot
- 2 inches of fresh ginger

Directions:

1. Wash all the fruit and vegetables. Core the apples cut into wedges. Peel and slice the ginger.
2. Tear beet greens and kale into pieces. Peel oranges and separate the segments.
3. First, add oranges into the juicer, followed by kale and apple. Next, add the beets, beet greens, and ginger, and lastly, add the carrot.
4. Pour into a glass and serve with crushed ice.

IRON BOOSTING JUICE

Difficulty: ★★☆☆☆

Preparation time: 5 minutes

Servings: 1

Ingredients:

- 1/2 cucumber
- 1 cups romaine lettuce
- 1 green apples
- 2 sticks celery
- 1 cup broccoli florets
- Juice of a lime

Directions:

1. Wash the vegetables and apples.
2. Chop cucumber into chunks. Tear the lettuce leaves. Slice celery into two-inch parts.
3. Place the broccoli, celery, lettuce, apples, and cucumber in a juicer.
4. Extract the juice and stir in lime juice.
5. Pour into glasses and serve.

CARROT APPLE BEET JUICE

Difficulty: ★★☆☆☆

Preparation time: 6 minutes

Servings: 1

Ingredients:

- 1 medium beets
- 1 apple
- 1/2 inch of fresh ginger
- 1/2 tablespoon honey or to taste
- 5 to 6 carrots
- one-eighth cup fresh lemon juice

Directions:

1. Wash vegetables and apples.
2. Peel and slice the ginger. Core the apples & chop them into portions. Trim the carrots and beets and chop them into chunks.
3. Place beets, apples, ginger, and carrots in a juicer and extract the juice.
4. Add lemon juice and honey.
5. Add some crushed ice and serve.

Immune Boosting Juices

Immune-boosting juices are becoming increasingly popular among health enthusiasts who are looking for a natural way to boost their immune system. These juices are made with a variety of fruits and vegetables that are high in vitamins and minerals, which are essential for preserving a healthy immune system.

The body's natural defense against harmful pathogens, such as viruses and bacteria, is the immune system. Maintaining a robust immune system is vital as it protects the body from illnesses and diseases. Nevertheless, various factors, including inadequate sleep, poor nutrition, stress, and toxin exposure, can weaken the immune system, rendering the body more susceptible to infections. To counteract this, immune-boosting juices can be consumed, as they contain vital nutrients, such as minerals and vitamins, that can help bolster the immune system and promote better health.

Immune-boosting juices offer a significant advantage due to their high concentration of antioxidants. Antioxidants are compounds that shield the body against harm from unstable molecules known as free radicals. These unstable molecules have the potential to damage cells and cause severe illnesses such as heart disease and cancer. Immune-boosting juices that incorporate fruits and vegetables such as berries, spinach, and carrots are great options due to their abundant antioxidant content.

Immune-boosting juices have a significant advantage in that they are abundant in vitamin C, a potent antioxidant that plays a crucial role in immune function. It promotes the generation of white blood cells, which are necessary for combating infections. Oranges, lemons, and grapefruits are examples of citrus fruits that provide abundant sources of vitamin C and are ideal for use in immune-boosting juices. Furthermore, immune-boosting juices are rich in other crucial vitamins and minerals, such as vitamin A, vitamin E, and zinc, which are crucial for preserving a robust immune system and safeguarding the body against diseases. Immune-boosting juices are an excellent way to strengthen the immune system and improve overall health. By incorporating ingredients such as berries, spinach, carrots, citrus fruits, and ginger, you can create delicious and nutritious juices that are packed with essential vitamins and minerals. So why not try making your own immune-boosting juice today? Your body will thank you!

SUPER IMMUNITY JUICE

Difficulty: ★★☆☆☆

Preparation time: 4 minutes

Servings: 1

Ingredients:

- 1 inches of fresh ginger
- 1 ½ large oranges
- 1 piece (2 inches) of fresh turmeric

Directions:

1. Wash ginger, oranges, and turmeric.
2. Peel the oranges and separate the segments.
3. Peel the ginger and turmeric and cut them into slices.
4. Place ginger, turmeric, and orange in the juicer and extract the juice.
5. Pour the juice into glasses and serve with ice.

MANGO AND GRAPEFRUIT JUICE

Difficulty: ★★☆☆☆

Preparation time: 5 minutes

Servings: 1

Ingredients:

- 1 grapefruit
- 1/2 inch fresh ginger
- 1 cup chopped mango
- 2 large carrots
- A pinch of cayenne pepper
- 1/8 teaspoon turmeric powder or ½ inch fresh turmeric

Directions:

1. Wash carrots, grapefruit, turmeric, and ginger.
2. Peel the grapefruit. Separate the grapefruit segments.
3. Peel the ginger and fresh turmeric if using and cut into slices.
4. Trim the carrots and chop them into chunks.
5. Place ginger, turmeric, carrots, grapefruit, and mangoes in a juicer and extract the juice.
6. Pour into glasses. Add turmeric powder if using, now, and stir.
7. Serve with crushed ice.

LEMON GINGER TURMERIC WELLNESS JUICE

Difficulty: ★★☆☆☆

Preparation time: 5 minutes

Servings: 1

Ingredients:

- 1 small oranges
- 1/4 cup sliced fresh turmeric
- one-eighth tsp. ground black pepper
- 2 small lemons
- 1/4 cup chopped fresh ginger
- 1/4 tsp. extra-virgin olive oil. (Elective but recommended)

Directions:

1. Wash the oranges, turmeric, lemons, and ginger well. Peel the ginger and turmeric if desired. Chop them up and measure them according to the ingredients list quantities.

2. Peel the orange and separate the segments. Peel the lemons and cut them into quarters.

3. Place oranges, turmeric, lemons, ginger, and turmeric in a juicer and extract the juice.

4. You can also blend the entire components inside a mixer till uniform.

5. Strain the juice. Add pepper and oil if using and stir.

6. Pour the juice into shot glasses and serve.

PEAR AND GRAPEFRUIT JUICE

Difficulty: ★★☆☆☆

Preparation time: 5 minutes

Servings: 1

Ingredients:

- 1 pear
- 1 lemon
- 2 slices of fresh pineapple
- 1/2-inch slice of fresh ginger
- 1 yellow grapefruit
- 1 stick celery

Directions:

1. Wash pears, lemons, pineapple, grapefruit, celery, and ginger.

2. Peel the lemons and grapefruit. Separate the grapefruit segments.

3. Peel the ginger and cut into slices. Chop the pineapple slices into chunks. Cut the celery into 2-inch pieces.

4. Core the pears and chop them into chunks.

5. Place pears, lemons, pineapple, ginger, grapefruit, and celery in a juicer and extract the juice.

6. Pour into glasses. Serve with crushed ice.

IMMUNE BOOSTER JUICE

Difficulty: ★★☆☆☆

Preparation time: 5 minutes

Servings: 1

Ingredients:

- 1/4 fresh pineapple
- 1/2 lemon
- 1 orange
- 1 inches of fresh ginger

Directions:

1. Wash the pineapple and oranges.
2. Peel the pineapple and chop it into chunks.
3. Peel the lemon and oranges. Separate the orange segments.
4. Peel the ginger and cut into slices.
5. Place pineapple, lemon, oranges, and ginger in the juicer and extract the juice.
6. You can also blend the components inside a mixer till uniform.
7. Strain the juice.
8. Pour the juice into glasses and serve with crushed ice.

SPICY MELON IMMUNE BOOSTER

Difficulty: ★★☆☆☆

Preparation time: 4 minutes

Servings: 1

Ingredients:

- 1/2 big yellow bell pepper
- 2 cups watermelon

Directions:

1. To prepare the items, you may have to skin, slice, de-seed, or slice them.

2. Put a bowl just below the outlet of the juicer.

3. Move the components across the juicer separately, following the sequence in which they are catalogued.

4. After stirring it, put the juice into the glasses to offer.

CARROT AND APPLE JUICE

Difficulty: ★★☆☆☆

Preparation time: 5 minutes

Servings: 1

Ingredients:

- 4 carrots
- 2 inches of fresh ginger
- 2 apples

Directions:

1. Wash trim carrots, ginger, and apples.

2. Trim and chop carrots into chunks.

3. Peel the ginger and cut into slices.

4. Core the apple and chop it into chunks.

5. Place apples, ginger, and carrots in the juicer and extract the juice.

6. Pour into glasses and serve with ice.

IMMUNE-BOOSTING PINEAPPLE AND SPINACH JUICE

Difficulty: ★★☆☆☆

Preparation time: 5 minutes

Servings: 1

Ingredients:

- 1 cup chopped fresh pineapple
- 5 ounces spinach
- 1/2 cup water
- 1 cucumber

Directions:

1. Wash cucumber and spinach well.
2. Place the pineapple, spinach, and cucumber inside a mixer. Add water & mix till uniform.
3. Strain the juice if desired.
4. Pour into glasses and serve with ice.

ZUCCHINI AND GRAPEFRUIT JUICE

Difficulty: ★★☆☆☆

Preparation time: 6 minutes

Servings: 1

Ingredients:

- 1 apple
- 1 lime
- 1/2 pear
- 1/2-inch slice of fresh turmeric
- 1 grapefruit
- 1 zucchini

Directions:

1. Wash apple, limes, pear, grapefruit, turmeric, and zucchinis.
2. Peel the limes and grapefruit. Separate the grapefruit segments.
3. Peel the turmeric and cut into slices.
4. Core the pear and apples and chop them into chunks.
5. Place pears, lime, turmeric, zucchini, grapefruit, and apples in a juicer and extract the juice.
6. Pour into glasses. Serve with crushed ice.

FRUITY IMMUNE BOOSTING MIX

Difficulty: ★★☆☆☆

Preparation time: 7 minutes

Servings: 1

Ingredients:

- 1/2 orange
- 1/2 cup papaya
- 1/2 firm pear
- 1/2-inch slice of fresh ginger root
- 1/4 large cucumber

Directions:

1. To prepare the items, you may have to skin, slice, de-seed, or slice them.
2. Put a bowl just below the outlet of the juicer.
3. Move the components across the juicer separately, following the sequence in which they are catalogued.
4. After stirring it, put the juice into the glasses to offer.

PEAR AND APPLE JUICE

Difficulty: ★★☆☆☆

Preparation time: 5 minutes

Servings: 1

Ingredients:

- 3 cups fresh spinach or kale
- 1 green apple
- 1/2 lemon
- 1/2 big cucumber
- 1 green pear

Directions:

1. Wash fruit and vegetables.
2. Core the apple and pear and cut them into pieces.
3. Peel the lemon. Chop cucumber into chunks.
4. Place spinach, apple, lemon, cucumber, and pear in a juicer and extract the juice.
5. You can also make the juice by adding the entire components inside a mixer. Mix till uniform.
6. Strain the juice. Pour the juice into a glass then serve.

APPLE, CELERY, AND PARSLEY JUICE

Difficulty: ★★☆☆☆

Preparation time: 5 minutes

Servings: 1

Ingredients:

- 1 apple
- 1 bunch parsley
- 4 sticks celery

Directions:

1. Rinse apples, parsley, and celery.
2. Core the apples & chop them into portions.
3. Cut celery into 2-inch pieces.
4. Chop parsley along with stems.
5. Place a few apples in the juicer. Next, add parsley, followed by celery.
6. Extract the juice. Now add the remaining apples and extract the juice.
7. Stir the juice and pour it into glasses.
8. Serve with ice.

MANGO ORANGE IMMUNE BOOSTER

Difficulty: ★★☆☆☆

Preparation time: 6 minutes

Servings: 1

Ingredients:

- 1/2 cup mango
- 1/2-inch slice of fresh ginger root
- 1 orange
- 1/4 large cucumber

Directions:

1. To prepare the items, you may have to skin, slice, de-seed, or slice them.
2. Put a bowl just below the outlet of the juicer.
3. Move the components across the juicer separately, following the sequence in which they are catalogued.
4. After stirring it, put the juice into the glasses to offer.

Digestion Juices

Juices have been a part of our diet for centuries. They are packed with essential nutrients that can help in maintaining a healthy body. While some juices are known for their energizing properties, others are known for their ability to improve digestion. A healthy digestive system is essential for overall health, as it ensures that nutrients are absorbed and waste is eliminated effectively.

Digestive issues are a common problem that affects people of all ages. Poor eating habits, stress, and a sedentary lifestyle are some of the factors that can lead to digestive problems. Digestive issues can range from simple problems like bloating and constipation to more severe problems like Irritable Bowel Syndrome (IBS) and Crohn's disease. However, including certain juices in your diet can help alleviate these symptoms and promote good digestion.

One of the best juices for digestion is Aloe Vera juice. For centuries, people have utilized Aloe Vera, which is a type of succulent plant, for its medicinal properties. It has enzymes that aid in the digestion of food and provide a soothing effect on the digestive tract. Drinking Aloe Vera juice regularly can help alleviate symptoms of heartburn, bloating, and constipation.

Another excellent juice for digestion is ginger juice. The anti-inflammatory properties of ginger can aid in decreasing gut inflammation. It also contains compounds that help in breaking down food and aids in digestion. Drinking ginger juice regularly can help relieve symptoms of nausea, bloating, and constipation.

Papaya juice is another excellent juice for digestion. Papaya contains enzymes called papain that help in breaking down proteins and aid in digestion. It also contains fiber that helps in regulating bowel movements. Drinking papaya juice regularly can help alleviate symptoms of bloating, constipation, and stomach pain.

Green juices are also great for digestion. They are packed with essential nutrients like vitamins, minerals, and fiber that help in maintaining a healthy digestive system. Green juices also contain chlorophyll, which can help reduce inflammation in the gut. Some excellent green juices for digestion include spinach juice, kale juice, and wheatgrass juice.

Lastly, Lemon juice is another excellent juice for digestion. The high content of vitamin C in lemons aids in enhancing the immune system. They also contain compounds that help in breaking down food and aid in digestion. Drinking lemon juice regularly can help alleviate symptoms of bloating and constipation.

Incorporating these juices into your diet can help improve your digestion and promote a healthy gut. It is important to note that while these juices are beneficial for digestion, they should not be used as a substitute for a healthy and balanced diet. Additionally, people with certain health conditions should consult with their healthcare provider before adding these juices to their diet.

BLOAT-REDUCING JUICE

Difficulty: ★★☆☆☆

Preparation time: 5 minutes

Servings: 1

Ingredients:

- 1 apple
- 1/2 cucumber
- 5 kale leaves
- 1 ½ - 2 sticks of celery

Directions:

1. Wash the apple and vegetables.
2. Core the apple and cut it into wedges. Chop the cucumber. Tear the kale leaves, and cut the celery into about 2-inch pieces.
3. Place apple, kale, celery, and cucumber in a juicer and extract the juice.
4. Put into a glass and serve with ice.

JUICE FOR UPSET STOMACH

Difficulty: ★★☆☆☆

Preparation time: 6 minutes

Servings: 1

Ingredients:

- 1/4 apple
- 1/2 small cucumber
- 1/4 beet
- 1/4 stalk celery
- 1/2-inch piece of ginger
- 1/4 tablespoon apple cider vinegar
- A small bunch of fresh mint

Directions:

1. Wash ginger, celery, cucumber, beet, and parsley. Peel ginger. Trim the beet and chop it into chunks.

2. Slice ginger and celery. Chop cucumber into chunks. Pick the mint leaves from the bunch. Core the apple and chop it into chunks.

3. First, put apple followed by celery in the juicer. Next, add mint and ginger followed by the celery, beet, and carrots. Finally, add cucumber and extract the juice. Add apple cider vinegar and stir. Taste the juice and dilute it with water if desired.

4. Pour into 1 glass and serve with crushed ice; add some more mint leaves if desired.

GOOD DIGESTION CELERY JUICE

Difficulty: ★★☆☆☆

Preparation time: 5 minutes

Servings: 1

Ingredients:

- 1/2 pound celery
- 1/4 large navel orange
- 1/2 large cucumber
- 1/2 tablespoon lemon juice

Directions:

1. Wash the celery, orange, and cucumber. Peel the orange and separate it into segments.

2. Peel cucumbers if desired, then chop the cucumber and celery into pieces.

3. Put the celery, orange, and cucumber in a juicer and extract the juice.

4. Include lemon juice & mix. Put into glasses & serve with ice.

PLUM AND PASSION FRUIT JUICE TO RELIEVE CONSTIPATION

Difficulty: ★★☆☆☆

Preparation time: 4 minutes

Servings: 1

Ingredients:

- 1 passion fruit
- 2 medium plums
- 1/2 tsp. fennel seed powder
- one-eighth tsp. salt
- 1/4 cup water

Directions:

1. Wash the fruit. Pit the plums. Scoop out the pulp from the passion fruit.

2. Add scooped passion fruit, plum, and water into a mixer & mix till uniform. Strain the juice. Include fennel seed powder and salt and stir well.

3. Pour into glasses and serve with crushed ice.

ALOE VERA JUICE

Difficulty: ★★☆☆☆

Preparation time: 5 minutes

Servings: 1

Ingredients:

- 1 medium cucumber
- 1/2 cup water
- 1/2 lemon juice
- 1 tablespoon fresh aloe Vera gel
- 1/2 inch fresh ginger

Directions:

1. Wash the cucumber and chop it into chunks. Peel and slice the ginger.

2. Take a piece of fresh aloe Vera juice and carefully slice off the thick outer part of the leaf. Inside the leaf, you will find the gel. Take a tablespoon of the gel & include it to a container.

3. Include lemon juice, cucumber ginger, and water and blend until smooth.

4. Strain the juice and add it back into the blender. Now add the aloe Vera juice and blend on low speed until smooth.

5. Serve.

JUICE FOR GUT HEALTH

Difficulty: ★★☆☆☆

Preparation time: 6 minutes

Servings: 1

Ingredients:

- 1/2 apple
- 1 small cucumber
- 2 medium carrots
- 1 small beet
- 2 sticks celery
- 1/2 small lemon
- A small bunch of parsley
- 1-inch piece of fresh ginger

Directions:

1. Wash ginger, celery, cucumber, lemon, beet, and parsley. Peel ginger. Trim carrots and beetroot and chop them into chunks.
2. Slice ginger and celery. Peel the lemon. Chop cucumber into chunks. Chop parsley. Core the apple and chop it into chunks.
3. First, add the apple followed by the celery in the juicer. Next, add parsley and ginger, followed by the lemon, beet, and carrots. Finally, add cucumber and extract the juice.
4. Pour into a glass and serve with crushed ice.

CABBAGE JUICE FOR ULCERS AND GASTRITIS

Difficulty: ★★☆☆☆

Preparation time: 4 minutes

Servings: 1

Ingredients:

- 1/2 red cabbage
- 1 lemon
- 1 green apples

Directions:

1. Wash the cabbage, lemons, and apples.
2. Core the apples then slice them into portions or wedges.
3. Skin the lemon. Shred the cabbage.
4. Place cabbage, lemons, and apples in the juicer and extract the juice.
5. Put into glasses and serve with ice.

THE CABBAGE JUICE FOR ACID REFLUX

Difficulty: ★★☆☆☆

Preparation time: 5 minutes

Servings: 1

Ingredients:

- 2 cups shredded purple cabbage
- Juice of a lemon
- 3 sticks celery

Directions:

1. Wash all the vegetables. Chop celery into 2-inch pieces.
2. Place cabbage, celery, and lemon juice inside a mixer & mix till uniform.
3. Strain the juice and pour it into glasses.
4. Serve.

RAW VEGGIES JUICE

Difficulty: ★★☆☆☆

Preparation time: 5 minutes

Servings: 1

Ingredients:

- 1 small beet
- 1 small cucumber
- 1 small tomato
- 1/2 cup spinach
- 1/2 cup cabbage
- 1/2 cup broccoli florets
- 1/2 cup parsley

Directions:

1. Wash all the vegetables.
2. Trim the beets and chop them into chunks.
3. Place beet, cucumber, spinach, cabbage, parsley, broccoli, and tomato in the juicer and extract the juice.
4. Put into a glass and serve with ice.

WATERMELON JUICE

Difficulty: ★★☆☆☆

Preparation time: 3 minutes

Servings: 1

Ingredients:

- 1 ½ cups watermelon cubes

Directions:

1. Do not remove the seeds from the watermelon.

2. Add watermelon cubes along with the seeds into a blender. Mix till uniform.

3. Put into a glass and serve with ice.

PINEAPPLE JUICE

Difficulty: ★★☆☆☆

Preparation time: 3 minutes

Servings: 1

Ingredients:

- 1/2 cup fresh pineapple chunks
- 1/2 cup water

Directions:

1. Add pineapple and water to a mixer. Mix till uniform.

2. Put into a glass and serve. This juice helps in colon cleansing if consumed in the morning.

CLEANSING ALOE VERA JUICE

Difficulty: ★★☆☆☆

Preparation time: 3 minutes

Servings: 1

Ingredients:

- 1 cup fresh aloe Vera pulp
- 1 tsp. fresh lemon juice

Directions:

1. Take a fresh leaf of aloe Vera. Remove the thick green part of the leaf on all the sides and remove the pulp.

2. Add aloe Vera pulp into a mixer & mix till uniform.

3. Put into a glass. Add lemon juice & stir.

4. Have this juice 2 to 3 times a day for effective colon cleansing.

FRESH GUAVA JUICE FOR ACID REFLUX

Difficulty: ★★☆☆☆

Preparation time: 5 minutes

Servings: 1

Ingredients:

- 1 cup peeled, diced guava
- 1/2 cup cold water
- 1 teaspoons sugar or honey or agave nectar
- 1/2-inch slice of fresh ginger

Directions:

1. Peel & slice the ginger. Add guava, water, sugar, and ginger into a mixer & mix till uniform.

2. Strain the juice. Put into glasses and serve with ice.

Bonus Smoothies

It is common for smoothies to be thick and creamy drinks made from a variety of puréed fruits and vegetables as well as a variety of other ingredients.

The most basic kind of smoothie calls for only two primary components: a base, and some kind of liquid. From that point on, you may mix and match the elements to your satisfaction.

The chilly, frosty smoothness of a milkshake is achieved in the final result by using frozen fruits and vegetables or ice cubes in several smoothie recipes. The taste profiles, on the other hand, might be quite different from one another depending on the components.

Typical ingredients

The following are common components used in homemade smoothies as well as those purchased from stores:

- Berries, bananas, apples, peaches, mangoes, and pineapples are some examples of fruits.
- Kale, spinach, arugula, wheatgrass, microgreens, avocado, cucumber, beetroot, cauliflower, and carrots are some of the vegetables that are used in this dish.
- Almond butter, peanut butter, walnut butter, flax meal, chia seeds, hemp seeds, and sunflower seed butter are some of the nut and available seed butter.
- Ginger, turmeric, cinnamon, cacao powder, cacao nibs, parsley, and basil are some of the herbs and spices that are used.
- Spirulina, bee pollen, powder, protein powder, and powdered versions of vitamin and mineral supplements are some examples of nutritional and herbal supplements.
- Water, fruit juice, vegetable juice, milk, non-dairy milk, coconut water, iced tea, and cold brew coffee are all examples of liquids.
- Maple syrup, raw sugar, honey, pitted dates, simple syrup, fruit juice concentrates, stevia, ice cream, and sorbet are some of the sweeteners that may be used.
- Other options include yogurt made from dairy or non-dairy products, cottage cheese, vanilla essence, soaked oats, cooked white beans, and silken tofu.

Types

The vast majority of smoothies may be placed under either one of the following categories or both, despite the fact that there is much overlap between them:

Fruit smoothies. This particular form of smoothie often consists of one or more kinds of fruit mixed with fruit juice, water, milk, or ice cream.

Smoothies made with greens. Blended with water, fruit juice, or milk, green smoothies include a variety of leafy green vegetables as well as fruit. Although they sometimes include a little amount of fruit for flavor, they typically include a greater proportion of vegetables than ordinary smoothies.

Smoothies made with protein. The foundation of a protein smoothie is often made up of one fruit or vegetable, a beverage, and a significant quantity of protein-rich ingredients such as protein powder, Greek yogurt cottage cheese, or silken tofu.

Bonus Smoothies

VANILLA CREAM AVOCADO SMOOTHIE

Difficulty: ★★★☆☆

Preparation time: 9 minutes

Servings: 1

Ingredients:

- 1/4 of an avocado
- 1/4 cup kale
- 1/2 tablespoon cacao nibs
- 1/4 cup Greek yogurt
- 1/4 cup vanilla almond milk
- 1/4 cup frozen mango
- 1 tsp. honey

Directions:

1. Add liquid first, then softer ingredients and harder items like ice or frozen fruit last.

2. Blend on medium and increase to high for 1 minute.

3. Repeat as necessary.

GRAPY SPINACH SMOOTHIE

Difficulty: ★★☆☆☆

Preparation time: 6 minutes

Servings: 1

Ingredients:

- 1/4 cup of cranberries
- 1/2 apple
- 1/2 cup grapes
- 1 cup of spinach
- 1/2 stalk of celery
- 4 ounces of water

Directions:

1. First blend the water, spinach, and celery to make your liquid vegetable base.

2. Include all the fruits & mix on high for 3 mins. Make sure that the smoothie has no chunks. Serve and enjoy this delicious drink.

Bonus Smoothies

GINGER AND TANGERINE SMOOTHIE

Difficulty: ★★☆☆☆

Preparation time: 5 minutes

Servings: 1

Ingredients:

- 1/4 cup pomegranate

- 1/2 inch ginger root, crushed

- 1/2 cup tangerine

- A pinch of Himalayan pink salt

Directions:

1. Toss the pomegranate, ginger roots and tangerine into your blender

2. Add a pinch of Himalayan salt

3. Serve chilled and relish!

Bonus Smoothies

BLACK PEPPER AND PINEAPPLE SMOOTHIE

Difficulty: ★★☆☆☆

Preparation time: 5 minutes

Servings: 1

Ingredients:

- 1/2 cup grapefruit, chopped
- 1/4 tsp. black pepper, freshly ground
- 1/2 cup pineapple, ripe
- A pinch of Himalayan pink salt

Directions:

1. Place every one of the components on the list into a mixer.

2. Mix the ingredients till you obtain a consistency that is silky uniform & creamy.

3. Present cold, & have fun with it!

Bonus Smoothies

COCOA BANANA SMOOTHIE

Difficulty: ★★★☆☆

Preparation time: 8 minutes

Servings: 1

Ingredients:

- 1 large bananas, peeled and sliced
- 1/8 cup creamy peanut butter
- 1/2 cup almond milk
- 1 tbsp. cocoa powder, unsweetened
- 1/4 tsp. vanilla extract
- 1/2 cup ice

Directions:

1. Place every one of the components on the list into a mixer.
2. Mix the ingredients till you obtain a consistency that is silky uniform & creamy.
3. Present cold, & have fun with it!

ALMOND BERRY SMOOTHIE

Difficulty: ★★☆☆☆

Preparation time: 7 minutes

Servings: 1

Ingredients:

- 1/2 cup cherries
- 1 cup fresh kale
- 2 tsps. honey
- 1/2 cup blueberries
- 1 cup almond milk

Directions:

1. Place every one of the components on the list into a mixer.

2. Mix the ingredients till you obtain a consistency that is silky uniform & creamy.

3. Present cold, & have fun with it!

AVOCADO WITH PINEAPPLE SMOOTHIE

Difficulty: ★★☆☆☆

Preparation time: 10 minutes

Servings: 1

Ingredients:

- 1/2 cup frozen pineapple portions
- 1/2 orange (skinned)
- 1/2 red bell pepper (sliced)
- 1/2 avocado (diced and frozen)
- 1/4 cup walnuts
- 3/4 cup water

Directions:

1. Put the pineapple, orange, bell pepper, avocado, walnuts, and water inside a mixer.
2. Mix on increased speed till uniform.
3. Divide evenly between 2 cups and enjoy!

Bonus Smoothies

CITRUS WITH CHIA SEEDS SMOOTHIE

Difficulty: ★★☆☆☆

Preparation time: 10 minutes

Servings: 1

Ingredients:

- 3/4 cup freshly embraced orange juice
- 1/8 cup pure mangos teen juice
- 3/4 cup frozen red raspberries
- 3/4 cup frozen peach slices
- 1/2 tablespoon chia seeds
- 1/2 tablespoon coconut oil, melted
- Few pinches of cayenne pepper, as required

Directions:

1. Add liquid initially, then softer components and harder items like ice last.
2. Blend on medium and increase to high for 1 minute.
3. Repeat as necessary.

Bonus Smoothies

FLAXSEED WITH STRAWBERRY SMOOTHIE

Difficulty: ★★☆☆☆

Preparation time: 8 minutes

Servings: 1

Ingredients:

- 2 fluid ounces coconut milk
- 1/3 cup fresh strawberries
- 2/3 tablespoon flaxseeds
- 1/3 Greek yogurt vanilla or coconut flavor (5.3 ounces)
- 1/4 teaspoon stevia (1 package)
- 1/3 cup ice cubes

Directions:

1. Turn on your mixer.
2. Mix all ingredients on increased speed for thirty-forty-five seconds, or 'til desired consistency is reached.

Conclusion

Whether you are searching for losing weight, detoxify your body, or simply improve your health, juicing is the way to go. You are undoubtedly familiar with the saying "an apple a day keeps the doctor away" and other clichés encouraging the consumption of fresh fruits and vegetables. We are only human, though, and sometimes we get bored with eating the same foods, especially the very healthy ones. If it has become a challenge to fit your daily servings of fruit and vegetables into your routine, juicing is the perfect solution. You can get an entire salad's worth of fresh produce into a single glass of sip-able juice.

Not only is juicing quick and easy, but it is also good for you! By replacing unhealthy meals with fresh-pressed juices that are loaded with vitamins and minerals, you can significantly improve your overall health. Once you stop loading down your body with toxins and additives, your body will begin to efficiently process nutrients, resulting in healthier hair, skin, nails, and organs. Additionally, you are also likely to experience improved digestion, and if it is your goal, healthy and sustainable weight loss. Juicing is a wonderful option for the whole family, so try out some of the delicious recipes in this book together and improve your health today.

Conversion Tables

Volume Equivalents (Liquid)

US Standard	US Standard (ounces)	Metric (approximate)
two tbsps.	1 fl. oz.	30 mL
quarter cup	2 fl. oz.	60 mL
half cup	4 fl. oz.	120 mL
one cup	8 fl. oz.	240 mL
one and a half cups	12 fl. oz.	355 mL
two cups or one pint	16 fl. oz.	475 mL

Volume Equivalents (Dry)

US Standard	Metric (approximate)
quarter tsp.	1 mL
half tsp.	2 mL
three-quarter tsp.	4 mL
one tsp.	5 mL
one tbsp.	15 mL
quarter cup	59 mL
one-third cup	79 mL
half cup	118 mL
two-third cup	156 mL
three-quarter cup	177 mL
one cup	235 mL

Weight Equivalents

US Standard	Metric (approximate)
one tbsp.	15 gram
half oz.	15 gram
one oz.	30 gram
two oz.	60 gram
four oz.	115 gram
eight oz.	225 gram
twelve oz.	340 gram
sixteen oz. or one lb.	455 gram

Printed in Great Britain
by Amazon

23869541R00073